ROASTING TIN COOKBOOK

Dive in with the comfort of knowing what fuels you, but always let flavor lead the way. Happy roasting!

The table of

CONTENTS

Quick and Easy: Here, you'll find recipes that demand minimal effort, perfect for busy weekdays. If you ever thought that roasting takes forever, this chapter will prove you wrong.

Around the World: Venture beyond your culinary borders and embark on a world tour, one roast at a time. Sample delicacies from different corners of the globe, all made in your trusty roasting tin.

Hearty Meat Roasts: Dive into the meaty world of roasting. From succulent chicken to tender beef, these roasts are perfect for when you're looking to serve something unforgettable.

Seafood Specials: If you're a seafood lover, this chapter is a treat. Discover how the roasting tin can transform ordinary seafood into a dish fit for royalty.

All-Day Breakfasts: Who said you can't roast breakfast? Whether you're an early riser or a brunch enthusiast, these recipes have got you covered.

Veggie Delights: For those who favor greens and grains, this chapter brings a range of vegetarian recipes that are both healthy and indulgent.

Sweet Treats: Roasting isn't just for savories. Dive into desserts that are roasted to perfection, ensuring you end your meal on a sweet note.

British Classics: Return to the roots with traditional British dishes. These classics have stood the test of time, and now they're given a roasting twist.

Hello, Tin-Tastic Enthusiast!

We've all been there – standing proud, admiring our culinary masterpiece, only to turn around and face the daunting mountain of dishes. Dread no more! The roasting tin is here to change the game. Your trusty kitchen companion promises minimal cleanup with flavor that packs a punch. It's a delightful journey back to basics, but with a sprinkle of modern charm.

Serving Size: Just Right for Two

All the recipes you'll encounter in this book are crafted for two. Planning a romantic date night? We've got you covered. Eating solo today and want to save some for tomorrow's meal? Consider it done. And for those occasions when you've got more mouths to feed or just fancy a bit less? Simply scale the servings up or down as per your need.

Foolproof Cooking, Flawless Eating

Before you get lost in the world of roasting tin recipes, here's a nugget of wisdom: each recipe has been crafted to be foolproof. We've all had our "oops" moments in the kitchen, so these dishes are here to guide you through, even on those days when the chef's hat feels a tad askew. Feel free to tweak and twist to match your tastes, serve with pride, and bask in the joy of minimal dish duty. Time to don those aprons and embark on this one-pan wonderland!

However, a small word of caution: these numbers are general estimates. Actual nutritional content might vary based on the exact ingredients you choose, the method you employ, or even the particular produce batch from the store. While we strive to offer a helpful overview, those of you keen on precise nutritional tracking (be it for macros or specific nutrients) might want to consult with a nutritionist or use a specialized recipe calculator.

Dive in with the comfort of knowing what fuels you, but always let flavor lead the way. Happy roasting!

ZESTY LEMON-HERB CHICKEN

When life gives you lemons, make this! A delectable mingling of tangy lemon slices and aromatic herbs caressing perfectly roasted chicken pieces, accompanied by vibrant, al dente veggies. It's a dance of flavors and aromas, all in less than 30 minutes.

INGREDIENTS

- 400g chicken breasts or thighs, boneless and skinless
- 2 tbsp olive oil
- 1 lemon, thinly sliced
- 2 tsp fresh rosemary, finely chopped
- 2 tsp fresh thyme, finely chopped
- 3 cloves garlic, minced
- 200g asparagus spears, trimmed
- 150g cherry tomatoes, halved
- Salt & pepper to taste

STEPS

1. Preheat: Start by preheating your oven to 425°F (220°C). Pop your roasting tin inside as well.
2. Marinate: In a bowl, combine olive oil, minced garlic, chopped herbs, salt, and pepper. Coat the chicken thoroughly.
3. Roast: Once the oven is hot, carefully remove the roasting tin and lay the chicken pieces in a single layer. Scatter the asparagus and cherry tomatoes around the chicken. Top each piece with lemon slices.
4. Cook: Slide the tin back into the oven and roast for about 20 minutes or until the chicken is golden and fully cooked through.

ALTERNATIVE

- Spice it up: Add a pinch of chili flakes or cayenne pepper for a kick.
- Citrus Swap: Replace lemon slices with thin slices of orange or lime for a different citrusy twist.
- Herb Garden: Swap rosemary and thyme with other herbs like basil or cilantro for a fresh taste.
- Veggie Variations: Swap out asparagus and cherry tomatoes for bell peppers or zucchini slices, depending on your preference.

QUICK-ROASTED VEGGIE MEDLEY

An explosion of colors and flavors, this dish offers a delightful journey through the Mediterranean, right in the comfort of your kitchen. Vibrant veggies, dressed with olive oil and aromatic herbs, roast to perfection in record time.

INGREDIENTS

- 200g cherry tomatoes, halved
- 200g bell peppers (a mix of red, yellow, and green), thinly sliced
- 150g zucchini, sliced into half-moons
- 150g red onion, thinly sliced
- 100g feta cheese, crumbled (optional)
- 2 tbsp olive oil
- 2 tsp dried oregano
- 1 tsp dried basil
- 1 garlic clove, minced
- Salt & pepper to taste

STEPS

1. Preheat with Precision: Preheat your oven to 450°F (230°C). As it warms up, place your roasting tin inside.
2. Toss it Together: In a large bowl, combine the veggies, olive oil, minced garlic, dried herbs, salt, and pepper. Toss well to ensure even coating.
3. Roast Away: Once preheated, carefully remove the roasting tin and spread the veggie mix in a single layer. This ensures quick and even roasting.
4. Cook to Perfection: Pop the tin back into the oven and roast for about 15-18 minutes, or until the veggies are tender and slightly charred. If using, sprinkle feta cheese over the veggies in the last 5 minutes of roasting.

ALTERNATIVE

- Go Greek: Add some pitted olives and swap out dried basil for some dried rosemary.
- Heat It Up: Toss in some chili flakes or sliced jalapeños for an extra kick.
- Crunch Time: For added texture, sprinkle some toasted pine nuts or slivered almonds in the final minutes of roasting.

SPICY SAUSAGE
& POTATO HASH

raving something hearty and spicy? Dive into this delectable hash, where spicy sausages meet crispy baby potatoes. The oven does the magic in just under 30 minutes, making this dish a quick fix for those spontaneous hunger pangs.

 ## INGREDIENTS

- 400g baby potatoes, halved or quartered depending on size
- 300g spicy sausage, sliced into rounds
- 1 red bell pepper, diced
- 1 medium red onion, diced
- 2 tbsp olive oil
- 1 tsp smoked paprika
- 1/2 tsp chili flakes (adjust based on heat preference)
- 2 garlic cloves, minced
- Salt & pepper to taste
- Fresh parsley or cilantro, finely chopped (for garnish)

 ## STEPS

1. Heat Up: Preheat oven to 450°F (230°C); place roasting tin inside to warm.
2. Mix & Marinate: Combine baby potatoes, sliced sausage, bell pepper, red onion, olive oil, smoked paprika, chili flakes, garlic, salt, and pepper. Coat well.
3. Roast: After preheating, remove hot tin; spread mixture in a single layer for even roasting.
4. Quick Cook: Roast 20-22 mins, stirring halfway, until potatoes are golden and sausage is cooked.
5. Garnish & Serve: Remove from oven, sprinkle with chopped parsley or cilantro before serving.

 ## ALTERNATIVE

- Veggie Version: Replace spicy sausage with a plant-based sausage or crumbled tofu marinated in spicy seasoning for a vegetarian twist.
- Heat Level: Adjust the amount of chili flakes or even incorporate a spicy chili sauce or paste for an extra kick.
- Herby Touch: Add rosemary or thyme for an aromatic infusion.

GARLIC BUTTER PRAWN

Delight Imagine the smell of sizzling garlic wafting through your kitchen, hinting at the juicy prawns roasting to perfection. Paired with sweet cherry tomatoes that burst with flavor, this dish is a symphony of taste that's done in a snap.

 ## INGREDIENTS

- 400g prawns, peeled and deveined
- 200g cherry tomatoes
- 4 garlic cloves, minced
- 100g unsalted butter, melted
- 1 tbsp fresh parsley, finely chopped
- 1/2 tsp chili flakes (optional, for some heat)
- 2 tbsp olive oil
- Salt & pepper to taste
- Lemon wedges, for serving

 ## STEPS

1. Heat Up: Preheat your oven to 450°F (230°C), placing the roasting tin inside as it warms.
2. Garlic Butter Mix: In a bowl, combine melted butter, minced garlic, chili flakes (if using), salt, and pepper.
3. Prawn Preparation: Toss the prawns and cherry tomatoes in the garlic butter mixture, ensuring they're well-coated.
4. Roast and Relish: Carefully remove the hot roasting tin from the oven. Spread the prawn and tomato mixture evenly across the tin. Return to the oven and roast for 10-12 minutes or until prawns are pink and tomatoes are slightly blistered.
5. Serve with Zest: Garnish with freshly chopped parsley and serve with lemon wedges for an added citrusy kick.

 ## ALTERNATIVE

- Garlic Herb Prawn: Replace the chili flakes with 1 tsp of dried oregano and 1 tsp of dried basil for an herb-infused variation.
- Citrusy Garlic Prawn: Add the zest of one lemon to the garlic butter mix for a zesty flavor twist. Serve with additional lemon wedges.
- Creamy Garlic Prawn Pasta: After roasting, toss the prawns and tomatoes with 200g of cooked spaghetti, adding 100ml of cooking cream to the mix. Stir well and serve immediately, garnished with extra parsley and freshly grated Parmesan.

HONEY-SOY
GLAZED SALMON

Let the ocean meet the orchard in this delightful blend of sweet and savory. Tender salmon fillets bathed in a glossy honey-soy glaze, with a sprinkle of sesame seeds, make for a meal that's as delectable as it is quick.

 ## INGREDIENTS

- 2 salmon fillets (about 150g each)
- 3 tbsp honey
- 2 tbsp soy sauce
- 1 garlic clove, minced
- 1 tsp ginger, freshly grated
- 1 tbsp olive oil
- 1 tbsp sesame seeds
- 2 green onions, thinly sliced (for garnish)
- 1/2 tsp chili flakes (optional, for added heat)

 ## STEPS:

1. Heat Up: Preheat your oven to 450°F (230°C), and don't forget to place the roasting tin inside to get it sizzling hot.
2. Glaze Goodness: In a bowl, mix together honey, soy sauce, minced garlic, grated ginger, and chili flakes (if using).
3. Prep the Salmon: Lightly brush the salmon fillets with olive oil on both sides. Pour the honey-soy mixture over the fillets, ensuring they're well-coated.
4. Roasting Right: Once your roasting tin is heated, remove it from the oven. Place the salmon fillets skin-side down and pour any remaining glaze over them. Return the tin to the oven and roast for 12-15 minutes or until the salmon easily flakes with a fork.
5. Garnish & Serve: Sprinkle the roasted salmon with sesame seeds and sliced green onions.

ALTERNATIVE

- Citrus-Honey Salmon: Add the zest and juice of one orange to the glaze mixture for a tangy twist on the sweet glaze.
- Honey-Teriyaki Salmon: Replace the soy sauce with teriyaki sauce for a different depth of flavor. Reduce honey by 1 tbsp due to the sweetness of teriyaki.
- Honey-Mustard Glazed Salmon: Mix in 1 tbsp of Dijon mustard with the honey and soy sauce for a piquant flavor contrast.

ROASTED CHICKPEA & FETA SALAD CRUNCH

meets zest in this vibrant dish! Imagine golden chickpeas with a crispy exterior but soft inside, mixed with creamy feta, and a symphony of fresh veggies. All topped off with a citrusy dressing for a burst of flavor.

 ## INGREDIENTS

- 400g canned chickpeas, drained, rinsed, and patted dry
- 150g feta cheese, crumbled
- 1 red bell pepper, diced
- 1 cucumber, diced
- 10 cherry tomatoes, halved
- 1/4 red onion, finely sliced
- 3 tbsp olive oil, divided
- 1 tsp smoked paprika
- Salt & pepper, to taste
- 2 tbsp lemon juice
- 1 garlic clove, minced
- 1 tsp dried oregano

 ## STEPS:

1. Heat Up: Preheat oven to 450°F (230°C) with a roasting tin inside.
2. Chickpea Chomp: Toss chickpeas with olive oil, smoked paprika, salt, and pepper. Spread on hot tin, roast 20-25 mins, shaking midway for even cooking, until golden and crunchy.
3. Vibrant Veggies: While chickpeas roast, mix red bell pepper, cucumber, cherry tomatoes, and red onion in a large bowl.
4. Zesty Dressing: Whisk 2 tbsp olive oil, lemon juice, garlic, oregano, salt, and pepper in a small bowl.
5. Combine & Crumble: Cool chickpeas slightly, add to veggies. Toss with dressing and top with crumbled feta.

 ## ALTERNATIVE

- Mediterranean Twist: Add in some chopped olives and replace the lemon juice with red wine vinegar for a Mediterranean flair.
- Green Goddess Chickpea Salad: Add in some chopped avocado and fresh parsley or cilantro. Use lime juice instead of lemon for the dressing.
- Spiced Roasted Chickpea Salad: For a spicier kick, sprinkle some cayenne pepper or chili flakes on the chickpeas before roasting.

TUSCAN TOMATO & BREAD SOUP

This is Tuscany in a tin! Dive into the comforting embrace of crunchy bread bathed in a tomato soup bursting with Italian flair. The olives and capers add that briny touch, while the herbs transport you straight to the rolling hills of Tuscany.

 ## INGREDIENTS

- 400g canned crushed tomatoes
- 2 cups day-old rustic bread, torn into chunks
- 1/4 cup black olives, pitted and sliced
- 2 tbsp capers, rinsed and drained
- 1 onion, finely chopped
- 2 cloves garlic, minced
- 4 cups chicken or vegetable broth
- 2 tbsp olive oil
- 1 tsp dried basil
- 1 tsp dried oregano
- 1/4 tsp red pepper flakes (optional, for a kick)
- Salt & pepper, to taste
- Fresh basil or parsley, for garnish

 ## STEPS:

1. Heat Up: Begin by preheating your oven to 450°F (230°C). Place your roasting tin inside to get it ready.
2. Sauté Away: In a bowl, mix onions, garlic, olive oil, dried basil, dried oregano, red pepper flakes, salt, and pepper. Transfer to the hot roasting tin and roast for 8-10 minutes, or until the onions are translucent.
3. Tomato Time: Add the crushed tomatoes, broth, olives, and capers to the tin, giving everything a good mix. Continue to roast for another 10 minutes, allowing the flavors to meld.
4. Bread Boost: Stir in the bread chunks, ensuring they're submerged in the broth. Roast for another 5-7 minutes or until the bread is soaked and slightly softened.
5. Serve & Garnish: Once out of the oven, let it sit for a couple of minutes to let the bread soak up even more flavor. Dish it out and garnish with fresh basil or parsley.

ALTERNATIVE

- Creamy Tomato Bread Soup: Swirl in 1/4 cup of heavy cream or coconut milk after the soup is done roasting for a creamier texture.
- Protein-Packed Soup: Add in some roasted chicken pieces or white beans for an extra dose of protein.
- Veggie-Loaded Tomato Soup: Stir in some chopped spinach, zucchini, or bell peppers along with the tomatoes for an added veggie boost.

BALSAMIC-GLAZED STEAK STRIPS

with Roasted Asparagus Unleash a culinary masterpiece from your oven in under 30 minutes! These steak strips, kissed by a balsamic reduction, are tender, flavorful, and perfectly paired with the earthy notes of roasted asparagus.

 ## INGREDIENTS

- 300g steak (sirloin or ribeye), cut into 1-inch strips
- 200g fresh asparagus, trimmed
- 1/4 cup balsamic vinegar
- 2 tbsp honey
- 2 tbsp olive oil, divided
- 3 cloves garlic, minced
- Salt & pepper, to taste
- 1/4 tsp red pepper flakes (optional for a kick)
- Fresh parsley or chives, finely chopped (for garnish)

 ## STEPS:

1. Heat Up: Preheat oven to 450°F (230°C), and place a roasting tin inside.
2. Asparagus Prep: Toss asparagus in 1 tbsp olive oil, salt, pepper, and garlic. Spread on hot tin; roast for 8 mins.
3. Steak & Glaze: Mix balsamic vinegar, honey, remaining olive oil, salt, pepper, and red pepper flakes. Coat steak strips, reserving excess glaze.
4. Sear & Roast: After asparagus roasts 8 mins, push aside. Place steak on tin, pour remaining glaze over. Roast 5-7 mins until desired doneness.
5. Garnish & Serve: Remove, garnish with chopped parsley or chives.

 ## ALTERNATIVE

- Zesty Orange-Balsamic Steak: Add 1 tbsp of orange zest and 2 tbsp of orange juice to the balsamic mixture for a citrusy twist.
- Vegetable Medley: Replace asparagus with a mix of bell peppers, zucchini, and cherry tomatoes for a varied veggie experience.
- Herb-Infused Steak: Mix in 1 tsp of dried rosemary or thyme to the balsamic glaze for a more herby aroma.

MEDITERRANEAN OLIVE & ARTICHOKE PASTA

Dive into the heart of the Mediterranean with this delectable oven-roasted pasta. Packed with briny olives, tender artichoke hearts, and a hint of citrus, this dish promises a burst of flavor with every bite.

 ## INGREDIENTS

- 200g penne pasta
- 1 cup black and green olives, pitted and roughly chopped
- 1 cup artichoke hearts, quartered
- 2 tbsp olive oil
- 3 cloves garlic, minced
- 1/4 cup fresh parsley, chopped
- Zest and juice of 1 lemon
- 1 tsp dried oregano
- 1/4 tsp red pepper flakes (optional for a kick)
- Salt & pepper, to taste
- Grated Parmesan or feta crumbles, for garnish
- Fresh basil or parsley, for garnish

 ## STEPS

1. Heat & Prep: Preheat your oven to 425°F (220°C) and place the roasting tin inside. Meanwhile, cook the penne pasta in boiling salted water until just al dente. Drain, reserving 1/4 cup of pasta water.
2. Sauce It Up: In a bowl, combine olives, artichoke hearts, olive oil, minced garlic, lemon zest, lemon juice, dried oregano, red pepper flakes (if using), salt, and pepper.
3. Mix & Roast: Remove the hot roasting tin from the oven. Toss in the pasta, the olive-artichoke mixture, and the reserved pasta water. Mix well to ensure the pasta is coated with the flavors. Roast in the oven for about 8-10 minutes, allowing the flavors to meld.
4. Garnish & Serve: Once out of the oven, sprinkle with fresh parsley or basil and your choice of cheese

 ## ALTERNATIVE

- Tomato Twist: Add a handful of halved cherry tomatoes to the mix before roasting for a fresh burst of sweetness.
- Protein Punch: Incorporate chunks of roasted chicken or sautéed shrimp for an added protein boost.
- Creamy Mediterranean Pasta: Drizzle in 1/4 cup of heavy cream or crème fraîche after roasting for a rich and creamy texture.

CAJUN SPICED CORN & BEAN CASSEROLE

Turn up the heat in your kitchen with this Southern-inspired casserole. Brimming with the richness of corn and beans, infused with robust Cajun flavors, and topped off with a cheesy crust, this dish is a festival of flavors and textures.

 ## INGREDIENTS

- 1 cup corn kernels (fresh or frozen)
- 1 can (15 oz.) black beans, drained and rinsed
- 1 can (15 oz.) kidney beans, drained and rinsed
- 1 bell pepper (preferably red or yellow), diced
- 1 onion, finely chopped
- 2 cloves garlic, minced
- 2 tbsp olive oil
- 2-3 tsp Cajun spice mix (adjust to taste)
- 1/2 cup tomato sauce or crushed tomatoes
- 1/4 cup vegetable broth or water
- Salt & pepper, to taste
- 1 cup grated cheddar or Monterey Jack cheese
- Fresh cilantro or green onions, chopped, for garnish

 ## STEPS:

1. Preheat & Sauté: Preheat your oven to 425°F (220°C) with the roasting tin inside. In a skillet, heat olive oil over medium heat. Add onions and garlic, sautéing until translucent.
2. Beans, Corn & Spice: Add the bell pepper, corn, black beans, and kidney beans. Stir in the Cajun spice mix, tomato sauce, and broth/water. Cook until everything is well-mixed and heated through.
3. Roast in Tin: Carefully transfer the mixture into the preheated roasting tin, spreading it evenly. Top with an even layer of grated cheese.
4. Bake & Garnish: Roast in the oven for about 10-12 minutes or until the cheese is bubbly and golden. Remove from the oven and let it sit for a couple of minutes before garnishing with chopped cilantro or green onions.

 ## ALTERNATIVE

- Protein Boost: Add diced chicken or ground turkey, sautéing it with the onions for a meaty twist.
- Creamy Casserole: Mix in 1/4 cup of sour cream or cream cheese before transferring the mixture to the roasting tin for a creamier texture.
- Veggie Variety: Incorporate diced zucchini or chunks of butternut squash for added flavor and nutrition.

FRENCH RATATOUILLE

Embark on a culinary journey to the French countryside with this classic dish. Featuring a medley of garden-fresh vegetables slow-roasted to caramelized perfection, the Ratatouille promises a symphony of flavors, reminiscent of sun-baked Provence.

 ## INGREDIENTS

- 1 zucchini, sliced into rounds
- 1 yellow squash, sliced into rounds
- 1 eggplant, sliced into rounds
- 1 red bell pepper, sliced into thin strips
- 1 yellow bell pepper, sliced into thin strips
- 1 onion, thinly sliced
- 3 cloves of garlic, minced
- 400g canned diced tomatoes or fresh tomatoes
- 2 tbsp olive oil
- 1 tsp fresh thyme leaves
- 1 tsp fresh rosemary, chopped
- Salt and pepper to taste
- Fresh basil for garnish

 ## STEPS

1. Heat & Prep: Preheat your oven to 180°C (350°F). Meanwhile, slice all the vegetables as described.
2. Layering: In a large roasting tin, start with a base of onions, garlic, and bell peppers. Drizzle with half of the olive oil and season. On this, arrange the zucchini, yellow squash, and eggplant rounds, followed by the remaining olive oil.
3. Season: Sprinkle the fresh herbs, and then pour the diced tomatoes, ensuring a good coat.
4. Roast: Slide the tin into the oven and let the veggies roast for about 45-50 minutes until tender and slightly caramelized.
5. Garnish & Serve: Cool slightly and garnish with fresh basil before serving.

 ## ALTERNATIVE

- Cheesy Ratatouille: Before the last 10 minutes of roasting, sprinkle grated Gruyère or mozzarella cheese for a gooey top.
- Ratatouille with Protein: Layer in slices of pre-cooked chicken breast or tofu for added sustenance.
- Herb Delight: Add a handful of chopped fresh cilantro or parsley before serving for an extra herbal kick.

MEXICAN ENCHILADA BAKE

Dive into the bold flavors of Mexico with this easy-to-prepare oven-roasted dish. Layers of soft tortillas, creamy beans, melted cheese, and a zesty sauce come together for a fiesta in every bite.

 ## INGREDIENTS

- 8 soft tortillas (corn or flour)
- 2 cups cooked black or pinto beans, mashed
- 1 cup corn kernels
- 2 cups enchilada sauce (store-bought or homemade)
- 2 cups shredded cheese (cheddar, Monterey Jack, or Mexican blend)
- 1 red bell pepper, diced
- 1 green bell pepper, diced
- 1 onion, finely chopped
- 3 cloves garlic, minced
- 1 jalapeño, finely chopped (optional for extra heat)
- 2 tbsp olive oil
- 1 tsp ground cumin
- 1 tsp chili powder
- Salt and pepper to taste
- Fresh cilantro, chopped (for garnish)
- Sour cream or Greek yogurt (for serving)

STEPS

1. Sauté Veggies: In a skillet, heat the olive oil over medium heat. Add onions, garlic, bell peppers, and jalapeño. Cook until softened, then add the spices (cumin, chili powder, salt, and pepper). Remove from heat and set aside.
2. Layer: In a large roasting tin, spread a thin layer of enchilada sauce. Place two tortillas side by side, slightly overlapping. Spread a layer of the mashed beans, followed by the sautéd veggies, corn, a sprinkle of cheese, and a drizzle of more sauce. Repeat the layers until all ingredients are used, finishing with a generous layer of cheese on top.
3. Bake: Preheat the oven to 375°F (190°C). Place the roasting tin in the oven and bake for about 25-30 minutes until the cheese is melted and slightly browned.
4. Serve: Let the enchilada bake rest for a few minutes after removing from the oven. Cut into squares, garnish with fresh cilantro, and serve with a dollop of sour cream or Greek yogurt.

 ## ALTERNATIVE

- Meaty Twist: Add a layer of cooked ground beef or shredded chicken for a non-vegetarian version.
- Green Enchilada Bake: Use green enchilada sauce and white cheese like queso fresco for a different flavor profile.
- Veggie Variation: Introduce roasted zucchini slices or mushrooms for an extra layer of vegetables.

JAPANESE TERIYAKI CHICKEN

Venture into the streets of Tokyo with this tantalizing teriyaki chicken. Perfectly roasted chicken pieces glazed with a luscious teriyaki sauce, boasting a harmonious blend of sweet and savory, and garnished with toasted sesame seeds for a delightful crunch.

 ## INGREDIENTS

- 400g chicken thighs or breasts, boneless and cut into bite-sized pieces
- 4 tbsp teriyaki sauce (store-bought or homemade)
- 2 tbsp soy sauce
- 2 tbsp mirin (sweet rice wine)
- 1 tbsp sake or white wine
- 2 tbsp honey or brown sugar
- 2 cloves garlic, minced
- 1 inch ginger, minced
- 2 tbsp sesame seeds, toasted
- 1 tbsp vegetable oil

 ## STEPS

1. Marinate & Infuse: In a bowl, mix the teriyaki sauce, soy sauce, mirin, sake, honey, garlic, and ginger. Add chicken pieces and coat them well. Marinate for at least 30 minutes.
2. Heat & Sizzle: Preheat your oven to 425°F (220°C). Heat the roasting tin inside. Once hot, add vegetable oil and the marinated chicken pieces, ensuring they are spread out in a single layer.
3. Roast & Glaze: Roast the chicken for 15-18 minutes, turning halfway through. For the last 5 minutes, baste with the remaining marinade for a glossy finish.
4. Garnish & Serve: Once cooked, remove from the oven and sprinkle with toasted sesame seeds.

 ## ALTERNATIVE

- Go Veggie: Swap chicken for firm tofu cubes. Press the tofu to remove excess moisture, marinate, and roast.
- Spicy Kick: Add a tablespoon of Sriracha or sliced red chili to the marinade for an extra kick.
- Noodle Medley: Serve over roasted udon or soba noodles tossed with thinly sliced green onions and a drizzle of sesame oil.

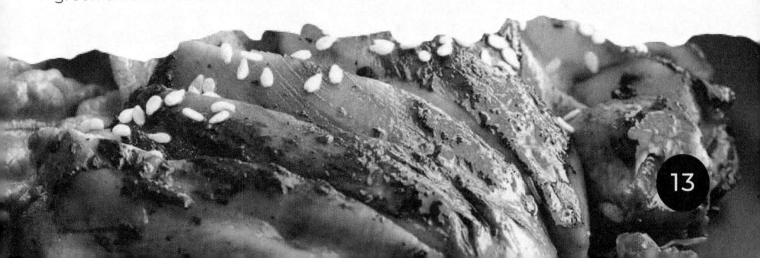

ITALIAN LASAGNA AL FORNO

Embrace the warmth of Italian kitchens with this classic Lasagna Al Forno. Layers of silky pasta enveloped in a creamy ricotta and spinach blend, all smothered in a rich marinara sauce. Each bite offers a comforting taste of Italy's culinary heritage.

 ## INGREDIENTS

- 9 lasagna sheets
- 400g ricotta cheese
- 200g fresh spinach, washed and roughly chopped
- 2 cups marinara sauce (store-bought or homemade)
- 2 cloves garlic, minced
- 200g mozzarella cheese, shredded
- 50g Parmesan cheese, grated
- 1 egg
- 2 tbsp olive oil
- Salt & pepper, to taste
- Fresh basil or parsley, for garnish

 ## STEPS

1. Prepare & Mix: Preheat your oven to 375°F (190°C). In a large bowl, mix the ricotta, chopped spinach, minced garlic, egg, salt, and pepper until well combined.
2. Layering Begins: Spread a thin layer of marinara sauce on the bottom of the preheated roasting tin. Place 3 lasagna sheets on top.
3. Ricotta Layer: Spread a third of the ricotta mixture over the lasagna sheets. Drizzle with some marinara sauce and sprinkle with mozzarella and Parmesan cheeses.
4. Repeat: Continue with the layering - lasagna sheets, ricotta mixture, marinara sauce, and cheeses. Do this until all ingredients are used up, finishing with a layer of cheese on top.
5. Bake & Relish: Cover the roasting tin with foil and bake for 25 minutes. Then, remove the foil and bake for an additional 10 minutes or until the cheese is golden and bubbly.
6. Serve: Once out of the oven, allow the lasagna to rest for 5 minutes. Garnish with fresh basil or parsley and slice to serve.

 ## ALTERNATIVE

- Meaty Layers: For a non-vegetarian twist, add cooked and crumbled Italian sausage or ground beef in between the layers.
- Cheesy Delight: Incorporate slices of provolone or fontina cheese for added richness and a gooey texture.
- Pesto Twist: Drizzle some basil pesto over the ricotta layers for an aromatic and herby flavor infusion.

THAI RED CURRY ROAST

Journey to the heart of Thailand with this fragrant roast, brimming with colorful vegetables and your choice of tofu or chicken. Bathed in a sumptuous coconut and red curry sauce, this dish offers a delightful blend of spice, sweetness, and creaminess.

 ## INGREDIENTS

- 200g firm tofu (cubed) or chicken breast (sliced)
- 1 red bell pepper, sliced
- 1 yellow bell pepper, sliced
- 1 zucchini, sliced into half-moons
- 1 carrot, julienned
- 200ml coconut milk
- 3 tbsp red curry paste
- 2 cloves garlic, minced
- 1 tbsp grated ginger
- 1 tbsp soy sauce
- 1 tsp brown sugar or palm sugar
- 2 tbsp vegetable oil or coconut oil
- Fresh basil or cilantro, for garnish
- 1 lime, cut into wedges, for serving

 ## STEPS

1. Curry Mix: In a bowl, whisk together coconut milk, red curry paste, soy sauce, and brown sugar until smooth.
2. Tofu/Chicken Prep: If using tofu, press it between paper towels to remove excess moisture. If using chicken, season with a pinch of salt.
3. Roasting Tin Magic: Preheat your oven to 400°F (200°C) and place the roasting tin inside. Once hot, add the vegetable or coconut oil, followed by garlic and ginger. Sauté for a minute.
4. Layer & Roast: Add the tofu or chicken pieces to the tin. Pour the curry mixture over, ensuring each piece is well coated. Add the vegetables, ensuring they are submerged in the sauce. Roast in the oven for 20-25 minutes, until the veggies are tender and the tofu/chicken is cooked through.
5. Serve: Garnish with fresh basil or cilantro and serve with lime wedges on the side.

ALTERNATIVE

- Green Curry Twist: Swap red curry paste with green curry paste for a different aromatic profile.
- Seafood Delight: Substitute tofu/chicken with shrimp or chunks of white fish for a seafood variation.
- Heat It Up: Add sliced red chili peppers or a touch of chili oil to the sauce for an extra kick of spiciness.

INDIAN TANDOORI PANEER

Immerse yourself in the rich culinary heritage of India with this tantalizing Tandoori Paneer roast. Soft, marinated paneer cubes meld beautifully with the smoky flavors of bell peppers and onions, reminiscent of traditional tandoor-cooked delicacies.

 ## INGREDIENTS

- 250g paneer, cut into cubes
- 1 red bell pepper, deseeded and cut into squares
- 1 green bell pepper, deseeded and cut into squares
- 1 large onion, cut into chunks
- 2 tbsp yogurt (preferably thick Greek yogurt or hung curd)
- 2 tbsp lemon juice
- 2 tsp ginger-garlic paste
- 1.5 tsp red chili powder (adjust according to heat preference)
- 1 tsp turmeric powder
- 1.5 tsp garam masala
- 1 tsp cumin powder
- 1 tsp coriander powder
- Salt, to taste
- 2 tbsp vegetable oil or ghee
- Fresh cilantro, for garnish
- Lemon wedges, for serving

 ## STEPS

1. Marination Magic: In a mixing bowl, combine yogurt, lemon juice, ginger-garlic paste, red chili powder, turmeric, garam masala, cumin powder, coriander powder, salt, and 1 tbsp oil. Mix well to form a smooth paste.
2. Paneer Prep: Toss the paneer cubes into the marinade, ensuring they're fully coated. Allow to marinate for at least 30 minutes, longer if possible.
3. Roasting Tin Ready: Preheat your oven to 425°F (220°C) and place the roasting tin inside. Once hot, add the remaining oil or ghee.
4. Layer & Roast: Scatter the marinated paneer cubes, bell peppers, and onions in the roasting tin. Ensure an even spread. Roast for 20-25 minutes, turning halfway, until the paneer is golden and the veggies are charred at the edges.
5. Serve: Garnish with fresh cilantro and accompany with lemon wedges.

 ## ALTERNATIVE

- Protein Shift: Swap paneer for tofu or chicken for a different protein choice.
- Smokey Twist: Add a drop of liquid smoke to the marinade for an intensified smoky flavor.
- Creamy Delight: Mix in 2 tbsp of heavy cream to the marinade for a richer, creamier texture.

MOROCCAN LAMB TAGINE

Embark on a culinary journey to the heart of North Africa with this aromatic Moroccan Lamb Tagine. Succulent lamb melds with the sweetness of apricots and the crunch of almonds, all elevated by a symphony of spices.

INGREDIENTS

- 300g lamb, cut into bite-sized chunks
- 1/2 cup dried apricots, halved
- 1/4 cup almonds, toasted and roughly chopped
- 1 onion, finely chopped
- 2 cloves garlic, minced
- 2 tbsp olive oil
- 1 tsp ground cumin
- 1 tsp ground ginger
- 1 tsp ground coriander
- 1/2 tsp ground cinnamon
- 1/4 tsp ground allspice
- 1/4 tsp cayenne pepper
- 2 cups chicken or vegetable broth
- Salt, to taste
- Fresh coriander, for garnish
- Lemon zest, for garnish

STEPS

1. Spice Infusion: In a bowl, mix together the cumin, ginger, coriander, cinnamon, allspice, and cayenne pepper. Coat the lamb chunks with the spice mixture.
2. Golden Start: Preheat your oven to 325°F (165°C) and place the roasting tin inside. Once hot, add olive oil. Add the lamb and sear until browned on all sides.
3. Flavor Foundation: Add chopped onions and minced garlic to the tin and cook until onions are translucent.
4. Mix & Simmer: Pour in the broth and add apricots. Stir everything together, ensuring the lamb is submerged. Cover the roasting tin with aluminum foil.
5. Oven Magic: Transfer the tin to the oven and let it cook for 2 hours or until the lamb is tender and the flavors melded.
6. Garnish & Serve: Once out of the oven, sprinkle with toasted almonds, fresh coriander, and lemon zest.

ALTERNATIVE

- Vegetable Variation: For a vegetarian twist, replace the lamb with chunks of butternut squash or eggplant.
- Fruit Fusion: Swap apricots for prunes or golden raisins for a different sweet note.
- Nutty Boost: Replace almonds with toasted pistachios or pine nuts for a varied crunch.

BRAZILIAN PICANHA ROAST

ive into the rich flavors of Brazil with this sumptuous Picanha Roast. Renowned for its tender texture and unmatched flavor, the top sirloin cap is seasoned simply with coarse salt to let the meat's natural flavors shine. Traditionally savored in Brazilian churrascarias, this dish invites you to a carnivorous carnival at your dining table.

INGREDIENTS

- 500g Picanha (top sirloin cap), keeping the fat cap intact
- 2-3 tbsp coarse salt (rock salt or sea salt)

Optional for serving:
- Lime wedges
- Chimichurri sauce or salsa verde

STEPS

Preparation Tips:
1. Ensure the Picanha is cut with the fat cap on for moisture and flavor.
2. Score the fat cap in a crisscross pattern without cutting into the meat.
3. Generously rub the meat with coarse salt on all sides.

Cooking Steps:
1. Preheat the oven to 475°F (245°C).
2. Sear the fat-side of the Picanha in a hot skillet until golden-brown (3-4 minutes).
3. Roast in the oven for 15-20 minutes for medium-rare (use a thermometer for 130°F or 54°C).
4. Let the meat rest for 10 minutes before slicing.
5. Serve with lime wedges and optional chimichurri sauce.

ALTERNATIVE

- Herbal Notes: Before roasting, sprinkle some chopped rosemary or thyme over the meat for added aroma and flavor.
- Spicy Kick: For those who enjoy a little heat, add a sprinkle of red pepper flakes or a dash of cayenne pepper alongside the salt.
- Garlic Lovers: Add minced garlic to the coarse salt rub for a garlic-infused Picanha experience.

VIETNAMESE LEMONGRASS PORK

Embark on a culinary journey to the vibrant streets of Vietnam with this fragrant lemongrass pork. Succulent strips of pork are marinated in an aromatic blend of lemongrass, fish sauce, and other seasonings, capturing the essence of traditional Vietnamese flavors.

 ## INGREDIENTS

- 500g pork tenderloin or pork shoulder, thinly sliced into strips
- 3 stalks lemongrass, finely minced
- 3 cloves garlic, minced
- 2 tbsp fish sauce
- 1 tbsp soy sauce
- 2 tsp sugar
- 1 tbsp vegetable oil or sesame oil
- 1 tsp ground black pepper

Optional for serving:
- Fresh cilantro
- Sliced red chilies
- Lime wedges
- Vermicelli noodles or rice

 ## STEPS

1. Marinate for Flavor: Combine minced lemongrass, garlic, fish sauce, soy sauce, sugar, oil, and pepper. Coat pork strips in the mix. Marinate 1 hr or overnight in the fridge.
2. Prep the Oven: Preheat to 425°F (220°C), place the tin inside.
3. Cook to Perfection: Remove marinated pork from fridge, let it reach room temp. Spread in tin, roast 15-20 mins until caramelized and cooked.
4. Serve with Flair: Transfer to a plate, garnish with cilantro, chilies, and lime wedges. Serve over noodles or rice.

 ## ALTERNATIVE

- Chicken Option: Swap out pork for chicken breasts or thighs for a lighter variation.
- Grill It: Instead of roasting, you can grill the marinated pork strips for a charred flavor.
- Sweet and Tangy: Add a splash of lime juice and a teaspoon of honey to the marinade for a zesty and sweet twist.

SOUTH AFRICAN BOBOTIE

Embark on a culinary journey to the vibrant streets of Vietnam with this fragrant lemongrass pork. Succulent strips of pork are marinated in an aromatic blend of lemongrass, fish sauce, and other seasonings, capturing the essence of traditional Vietnamese flavors.

 ## INGREDIENTS

- 250g ground beef or lamb
- 1 slice of bread, soaked in milk
- 1 small onion, finely chopped
- 1 clove garlic, minced
- 1 tbsp curry powder
- 1/2 tsp turmeric
- 1/2 tsp ground coriander
- 1 tbsp chutney or apricot jam
- 1 tbsp raisins or sultanas
- 1 bay leaf
- Salt & pepper, to taste

For the Topping:
- 1 large egg
- 75ml milk
- A pinch of turmeric or saffron (for color)

 ## STEPS

1. Preparation: Preheat oven to 180°C (350°F) and grease a suitable-sized roasting tin for two servings.
2. Meat Mix: Sauté onion and garlic until translucent. Add ground meat, cook until browned. Add curry powder, turmeric, coriander, chutney/jam, and raisins. Mix. Crumble bread slice into meat, stir well, season.
3. Transfer to Tin: Place mixture in tin, press to form an even layer.
4. Egg Topping: Whisk egg, milk, and turmeric/saffron. Pour over meat in tin.
5. Bake: Add bay leaf on top, bake for 20-25 mins until egg topping is set and golden.
6. Serve: Remove from oven, let it rest before serving.

 ## ALTERNATIVE

- Fruity Variation: Add a handful of diced apricots to the meat mixture for a sweeter touch.
- Veggie Bobotie: Replace the meat with a mixture of lentils and finely chopped mushrooms for a vegetarian version.

ARGENTINIAN CHIMICHURRI CHICKEN

Journey to the vibrant heart of Argentina with this tantalizing Chimichurri Chicken. Roasted to perfection in a tin, the succulent chicken harmonizes with the herbaceous chimichurri sauce, offering a symphony of flavors that dance on the palate.

 ## INGREDIENTS

- 2 chicken breasts (approx. 500g total)
- 2 tbsp olive oil
- Salt and pepper, to taste

For the Chimichurri Sauce:

- 1 cup fresh parsley, finely chopped
- 4 cloves garlic, minced
- 1/2 cup olive oil
- 3 tbsp red wine vinegar
- 1 tsp dried oregano
- 1/4 tsp red pepper flakes
- Salt and pepper, to taste

 ## STEPS

1. Prep & Marinate: Rub chicken breasts with olive oil, salt, and pepper. Allow it to marinate for at least 20 minutes for the flavors to meld. Meanwhile, prepare the chimichurri sauce by combining all sauce ingredients in a bowl. Mix well and set aside.
2. Roast the Chicken: Preheat your oven to 425°F (220°C). Place the marinated chicken breasts in the roasting tin. Roast for about 20-25 minutes or until the chicken is cooked through.
3. Serve with Flair: Once roasted, remove the chicken from the oven and immediately drizzle with a generous amount of chimichurri sauce. Reserve some sauce for serving on the side.
4. Plating: Slice the chicken and plate it up, drizzling extra sauce if desired. Pair with roasted vegetables or a fresh salad.

 ## ALTERNATIVE

- Zesty Twist: Add zest and juice of one lemon to the chimichurri sauce for an added tang.
- Heat it Up: Incorporate finely chopped fresh jalapeños or chili pepper for an extra kick.
- Herb Variations: Experiment by adding fresh cilantro or mint to the chimichurri sauce for a different herby note.

LEBANESE SHISH TAOUK

Experience the warmth of the Middle East with this traditional Lebanese Shish Taouk. Juicy chicken pieces, marinated in a tangy yogurt blend and roasted to perfection, bring forth an explosion of flavors that's nothing short of a Levantine treat.

 ## INGREDIENTS

- 300g chicken breast or thighs, cut into bite-sized pieces
- 1/2 cup plain yogurt
- 3 cloves garlic, minced
- 1 tbsp lemon juice
- 1 tbsp tomato paste
- 1 tsp paprika
- 1/2 tsp ground turmeric
- 1/2 tsp ground cumin
- 1/4 tsp cayenne pepper (optional for heat)
- Salt and pepper, to taste
- 2 tbsp olive oil

 ## STEPS

1. Marinate: Combine yogurt, garlic, lemon juice, tomato paste, spices, olive oil, salt, and pepper for a smooth marinade. Coat chicken pieces well, marinate for 2 hours or overnight in the fridge.
2. Preheat Oven & Prep Tin: Heat oven to 425°F (220°C). Let chicken reach room temp for 20 mins. Spread evenly in a roasting tin.
3. Roast: Roast chicken for 20-25 mins until fully cooked and slightly charred.
4. Serve: After cooking, rest briefly. Enjoy with garlic sauce or tahini, or both, traditionally.

ALTERNATIVE

- Skewer Style: Instead of roasting tin style, you can thread the marinated chicken pieces onto skewers and grill them.
- Veggie Additions: You can add bell peppers and onions to the marinade and roast them along with the chicken for a fuller meal.
- Spice Variations: Adjust the spices as per your preference; add a little ground coriander or allspice for a different flavor twist.

HAWAIIAN HULI HULI CHICKEN

Transport your senses to the tropical islands of Hawaii with this delectable Huli Huli Chicken. Juicy chicken roasted in a sweet and tangy pineapple-soy glaze embodies the spirit of Aloha in every bite.

 ## INGREDIENTS

- 300g chicken thighs or breasts
- 1/4 cup pineapple juice
- 2 tbsp soy sauce
- 2 tbsp brown sugar or honey
- 2 tbsp ketchup
- 1 tbsp rice vinegar
- 1 tbsp ginger, minced
- 2 cloves garlic, minced
- 1 tbsp sesame oil
- Salt and pepper, to taste
- Optional garnish: chopped green onions, sesame seeds

 ## STEPS

1. Marinate: Combine pineapple juice, soy sauce, brown sugar/honey, ketchup, rice vinegar, ginger, garlic, sesame oil, salt, and pepper. Reserve 1/4 cup for glazing. Coat chicken and marinate for 1 hour or overnight.
2. Preheat Oven & Prep Tin: Heat oven to 425°F (220°C). Let chicken sit at room temperature for 20 mins. Place chicken in a roasting tin, ensuring even spacing.
3. Roast: Roast for 20 mins. Baste with reserved marinade, then roast for 10-15 mins until caramelized and fully cooked.
4. Serve: Rest chicken, garnish with green onions and sesame seeds if desired, then serve.

 ## ALTERNATIVE

- Pineapple Pieces: You can add chunks of pineapple to the roasting tin for an enhanced tropical flavor.
- Heat Element: Introduce a little heat by adding crushed red pepper flakes to the marinade.
- Sides: Serve the Huli Huli chicken with coconut rice or a refreshing Hawaiian macaroni salad to round out the meal.

TURKISH IMAM BAYILDI

Immerse yourself in the rich culinary tapestry of Turkey with Imam Bayildi. This iconic dish features tender eggplants, stuffed with a vibrant mixture of tomatoes and onions, embodying the warmth and hospitality of Turkish cuisine.

INGREDIENTS

- 2 medium eggplants
- 2 tomatoes, finely diced
- 1 large onion, thinly sliced
- 3 cloves garlic, minced
- 1/4 cup olive oil, divided
- 1 tsp ground cumin
- 1 tsp paprika
- 1/2 tsp ground coriander
- Salt and pepper, to taste
- Fresh parsley, chopped (for garnish)
- Optional: 1 tbsp pine nuts or currants

STEPS

1. Prepare Eggplants: Preheat your oven to 400°F (200°C). Halve the eggplants lengthwise, keeping the stem. Scoop out the center, leaving a 1/4-inch shell. Chop the scooped-out flesh.
2. Sauté Filling: Heat half the olive oil in a skillet over medium heat. Sauté onions until translucent, then add garlic, diced tomatoes, chopped eggplant, cumin, paprika, coriander, salt, and pepper. Cook until soft. Add pine nuts or currants if desired.
3. Stuff & Roast: Brush or drizzle the eggplant shells with remaining olive oil. Fill with the tomato-onion mixture. Arrange in a roasting tin.
4. Bake: Cover with foil and bake at 400°F for 40 mins or until eggplants are tender.
5. Serve: Let cool, garnish with fresh parsley, and serve.

ALTERNATIVE

- Herb Infusion: Enhance the freshness by adding chopped fresh basil or mint to the tomato-onion mixture.
- Cheesy Delight: Before baking, sprinkle some crumbled feta or grated mozzarella on top of the stuffed eggplants for a delightful cheesy twist.
- Protein Boost: For a more hearty dish, add ground lamb or beef to the tomato-onion mixture. Adjust the cooking time accordingly.

CAMBODIAN AMOK

Embark on a culinary journey to Cambodia with this traditional Amok. Tender pieces of fish or tofu are enveloped in a rich and aromatic coconut curry, infused with lemongrass, kaffir lime leaves, and galangal. Steamed to perfection in a roasting tin, it offers a comforting taste of Southeast Asian cuisine.

INGREDIENTS

- 400g firm white fish fillets (like cod, snapper) or firm tofu, cut into bite-sized pieces
- 1 can (400ml) coconut milk
- 2 stalks lemongrass, finely minced (white parts only)
- 2 kaffir lime leaves, finely chopped
- 1 thumb-sized piece of galangal (or ginger), minced
- 2 cloves garlic, minced
- 1 small red chili (adjust to your heat preference), finely chopped
- 1 tsp turmeric powder
- 1 tbsp fish sauce (or soy sauce for a vegetarian version)
- 1 tsp palm sugar or brown sugar
- Salt, to taste
- Fresh cilantro, for garnish

STEPS

1. Marinate the Star Ingredient: In a large bowl, combine the fish or tofu with half of the coconut milk, lemongrass, kaffir lime leaves, galangal, garlic, chili, turmeric, fish sauce, and sugar. Mix well, ensuring every piece is well coated. Allow it to marinate for at least 30 minutes.
2. Roasting Tin Preparation: Preheat your oven to 375°F (190°C). Pour the marinated fish or tofu mixture into a roasting tin, spreading it out evenly. Drizzle the remaining coconut milk over the top.
3. Bake to Perfection: Cover the roasting tin with aluminum foil to lock in the moisture. Place the tin in the oven and bake for about 20-25 minutes or until the fish is cooked through and flakes easily with a fork (or the tofu is heated through). If using fish, ensure it doesn't overcook.
4. Final Touch: Once cooked, remove from the oven. Adjust the seasoning if needed. Garnish with fresh cilantro.

ALTERNATIVE

- Vegetable Add-ins: Introduce some additional texture by adding bell peppers, zucchini, or mushrooms to the curry.
- Meat Variation: If you're not into fish or tofu, chicken breast or thigh pieces can be a good substitute.
- Heat Levels: Adjust the spiciness by adding more or fewer chilies. For those who prefer milder flavors, deseed the chili or opt for a mild variety.

FINNISH SALMON SOUP

Delve into the heart of Finnish cuisine with this comforting salmon soup, traditionally known as "Lohikeitto." Tender chunks of salmon swim alongside hearty potatoes in a creamy broth, all elevated with a hint of fresh dill. Adapted for the roasting tin, this recipe retains its traditional flavor while simplifying the cooking process.

 ## INGREDIENTS

- 300g fresh salmon fillets, skin removed and cut into bite-sized cubes
- 2 medium potatoes, peeled and diced into 1-inch cubes
- 1 small onion, finely chopped
- 1 leek (white part only), thinly sliced
- 2 cups fish or vegetable stock
- 1 cup heavy cream
- 1 tbsp unsalted butter
- 2 tbsp fresh dill, finely chopped
- Salt and white pepper, to taste
- Lemon wedges and additional dill for serving

 ## STEPS

1. Roasting Tin Preparation: Preheat your oven to 375°F (190°C). In your roasting tin, scatter the diced potatoes, chopped onion, and sliced leek. Dot with butter and pour in the fish or vegetable stock.
2. Initial Roast: Cover the roasting tin with aluminum foil and place it in the oven. Bake for about 20 minutes, or until the potatoes are almost tender.
3. Add the Salmon: Remove the roasting tin from the oven, take off the foil, and carefully mix in the salmon cubes and heavy cream. Season with salt and white pepper, then return the tin to the oven (without the foil) for another 10-12 minutes, or until the salmon is cooked through and the soup is hot.
4. Final Touches: Once out of the oven, stir in the fresh dill. Adjust seasoning if necessary.
5. Serve Warm: Ladle the soup into bowls. Serve with lemon wedges and a sprinkle of extra dill on top.

 ## ALTERNATIVE

- Veggie Boost: Add finely sliced carrots or celery for added texture and nutrition.
- Herb Variations: Apart from dill, try other herbs like parsley or chervil for a different flavor profile.
- Lighter Version: If you prefer a lighter soup, substitute half or all of the heavy cream with milk or a dairy-free alternative.

HERB-CRUSTED LAMB ROAST

Delight in the simplicity and flavor of this herb-crusted lamb roast. Tender lamb enhanced with the aromatic trio of rosemary, thyme, and garlic guarantees a delectable dining experience. Adapted for the roasting tin, this recipe marries convenience with traditional flavors.

 ## INGREDIENTS

- 400g lamb roast
- 2 tbsp olive oil
- 1 tsp rosemary, minced
- 1 tsp thyme, minced
- 2 garlic cloves, minced
- Salt and pepper to taste

 ## STEPS

1. Roasting Tin Preparation: Preheat your oven to 400°F (200°C). Rub the lamb roast with olive oil, minced herbs, garlic, salt, and pepper. Place the seasoned lamb in the roasting tin.
2. Roasting Perfection: Roast the lamb in the preheated oven for approximately 25-30 minutes for medium-rare, or until it reaches your desired level of doneness. Adjust cooking time accordingly for rarer or more well-done preferences.
3. Rest & Serve: Once roasted, remove the lamb from the oven and let it rest for about 10 minutes. This allows the juices to redistribute, ensuring a moist cut. Slice the lamb thinly and serve.

 ## ALTERNATIVE

- Spice It Up: Introduce a touch of heat with a sprinkle of red chili flakes.
- Citrus Zest: Add lemon or orange zest for a refreshing citrus twist.
- Wine Reduction: After roasting, deglaze the tin with some red wine and cook it down to form a rich sauce to drizzle over the sliced lamb.

HONEY GLAZED PORK LOIN

Indulge in the succulence of this honey glazed pork loin, where the natural sweetness of honey pairs impeccably with savory pork. This roasting tin version streamlines the process, delivering a caramelized exterior and juicy interior.

 ## INGREDIENTS

 ## STEPS

- 400g pork loin
- 3 tbsp honey
- 2 tbsp soy sauce
- 1 tbsp olive oil
- 2 garlic cloves, minced
- 1 tsp dried rosemary or thyme (or fresh, finely chopped)
- Salt and pepper to taste

1. Marinate for Depth: In a bowl, whisk together honey, soy sauce, olive oil, minced garlic, and herbs. Season the pork loin with salt and pepper, then pour over the marinade, ensuring the pork is well coated. Allow it to marinate for at least 30 minutes, or overnight for better flavor infusion.
2. Roasting Tin Preparation: Preheat your oven to 375°F (190°C). Place the marinated pork loin into the roasting tin.
3. Glaze & Roast: Pour any remaining marinade over the pork. Roast in the preheated oven for about 30-35 minutes or until the internal temperature reaches 145°F (63°C). During the last 10 minutes of roasting, baste the pork with the juices in the tin for a shiny glaze.
4. Rest & Serve: After roasting, remove the pork loin from the oven and let it rest for 10 minutes, allowing the juices to settle. Slice and serve.

 ## ALTERNATIVE

- Spice Kick: Introduce some warmth by adding a pinch of ground ginger or cinnamon to the marinade.
- Citrus Note: Introduce a splash of orange or lemon juice to the marinade for a bright, tangy contrast.
- Searing First: For an extra layer of flavor, quickly sear the pork loin in a hot skillet before placing it in the roasting tin and proceeding with the oven roast.

BALSAMIC ROASTED BEEF FOR ROASTING TIN

Experience the symphony of flavors with this balsamic roasted beef. The tangy depth of balsamic vinegar harmonizes with the richness of beef, creating a meal that's both bold and refined. Simplified for the roasting tin, this recipe ensures a tantalizing crust and tender inside.

 ## INGREDIENTS

- 400g beef roast (like sirloin or rump)
- 3 tbsp balsamic vinegar
- 2 tbsp olive oil
- 2 garlic cloves, minced
- 1 tsp dried rosemary or thyme (or fresh, finely chopped)
- Salt and pepper to taste

 ## STEPS

1. Marinate & Infuse: In a bowl, combine balsamic vinegar, olive oil, minced garlic, and herbs. Season the beef with salt and pepper, then immerse it in the marinade. Allow to sit for at least 30 minutes, but for a deeper flavor, consider marinating overnight.
2. Roasting Tin & Oven Prep: Preheat your oven to 375°F (190°C). Position the marinated beef in the roasting tin.
3. Roast to Perfection: Drizzle any leftover marinade over the beef. Roast in the oven for about 30-40 minutes or until your desired level of doneness is achieved. For medium-rare, aim for an internal temperature of 130-135°F (54-57°C).
4. Rest & Slice: After roasting, remove the beef from the oven. Allow it to rest for about 10 minutes to redistribute the juices. Slice against the grain and serve.

ALTERNATIVE

- Herb Infusion: Replace dried herbs with a fresh herb bouquet tied with kitchen twine for a fresher aroma and flavor.
- Sweeter Edge: For a hint of sweetness, mix a tablespoon of honey or maple syrup into the marinade.
- Wine Deglaze: After roasting, use red wine to deglaze the roasting tin on the stove, scraping up any caramelized bits. Simmer until reduced by half, then drizzle over the sliced beef as a rich sauce.

SPICY HARISSA CHICKEN THIGHS FOR ROASTING TIN

Dive into a world of fiery flavors with these spicy harissa chicken thighs. The North African chili paste, harissa, brings a smoky depth and heat, elevating the humble chicken thigh to an exotic delight. Perfectly adapted for the roasting tin, this dish is both easy to prepare and brimming with flavor.

 ## INGREDIENTS

- 4 chicken thighs (about 400g), bone-in and skin-on
- 3 tbsp harissa paste
- 2 tbsp olive oil
- 1 tbsp lemon juice
- 2 garlic cloves, minced
- Salt and pepper to taste
- Fresh cilantro or parsley, chopped (for garnish)

 ## STEPS

1. Marinate for Depth: In a mixing bowl, combine harissa paste, olive oil, lemon juice, and minced garlic. Season the chicken thighs with salt and pepper and then coat them generously with the harissa mixture. Allow to marinate for at least 30 minutes, or for a richer flavor, marinate overnight in the refrigerator.
2. Roasting Tin & Oven Prep: Preheat your oven to 375°F (190°C). Arrange the marinated chicken thighs, skin side up, in the roasting tin.
3. Roast to Crispness: Bake the chicken in the oven for about 35-40 minutes, or until the skin is crispy and the chicken is cooked through, reaching an internal temperature of 165°F (74°C).
4. Garnish & Serve: Once out of the oven, sprinkle with freshly chopped cilantro or parsley for added freshness. Serve warm.

ALTERNATIVE

- Creamy Balance: Serve with a dollop of yogurt or tzatziki to counterbalance the heat.
- Veggie Mix: Before roasting, scatter a mixture of bell peppers, red onions, and cherry tomatoes around the chicken for a more complete meal.
- Lemon Boost: Add lemon slices or wedges to the roasting tin for an intensified citrusy aroma and flavor.

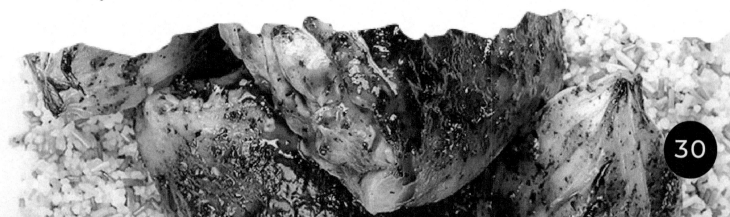

ROSEMARY GARLIC PRIME RIB

Celebrate a classic with this rosemary garlic prime rib. The fragrant aroma of rosemary combined with the punchy flavor of garlic elevates this prime rib, making it a feast for the senses. Designed for the roasting tin, this recipe guarantees a juicy, flavorful result with minimal fuss.

 ## INGREDIENTS

- 500g prime rib roast, boneless
- 4 garlic cloves, minced
- 2 tbsp fresh rosemary, finely chopped
- 2 tbsp olive oil
- Salt and freshly ground black pepper to taste
- 1/2 cup beef stock or red wine (for deglazing)

 ## STEPS

1. Prime Rib Prep: Combine minced garlic, chopped rosemary, olive oil, salt, and pepper to make a paste. Rub it over the prime rib, ensuring even coverage. Marinate for 30 minutes or overnight in the fridge for richer flavors.
2. Preheat & Place: Preheat your oven to 375°F (190°C). Set the marinated prime rib in a roasting tin.
3. Roast to Perfection: Roast in the oven for 40-50 minutes for medium-rare, adjusting for your preferred doneness. Keep in mind, the internal temperature rises slightly after cooking.
4. Rest & Deglaze: After roasting, rest the prime rib for 15 minutes. In the roasting tin, heat beef stock or red wine over low heat to deglaze, scraping up flavorful bits. This makes a simple jus or sauce.
5. Serve Slices: Slice the prime rib, drizzle with pan juices, and serve promptly.

ALTERNATIVE

- Herb Variations: Thyme or sage can be added or used in place of rosemary for a different aromatic touch.
- Mustard Kick: Mix in a tablespoon of Dijon mustard to the rub for an added layer of flavor.
- Veggie Roast: Surround the prime rib with root vegetables like carrots, parsnips, and potatoes in the roasting tin for a one-pan meal. Adjust roasting time accordingly.

LEMON BUTTER ROAST TURKEY BREAST

Dive into the zesty freshness of this lemon butter roast turkey breast. The citrusy undertones of lemon paired with melt-in-your-mouth butter ensure each slice is succulent and bursting with flavor. Tailored for the roasting tin, you get an impeccable main dish with the simplicity of one-pan cooking.

 ## INGREDIENTS

- 500g turkey breast, boneless and skin-on
- 4 tbsp unsalted butter, softened
- Zest and juice of 1 large lemon
- 2 garlic cloves, minced
- 1 tbsp fresh parsley, chopped
- Salt and freshly ground black pepper to taste

 ## STEPS

1. Lemony Butter Mixture: In a bowl, combine the softened butter, lemon zest, lemon juice, minced garlic, chopped parsley, salt, and pepper. Mix until well combined.
2. Prep the Turkey: Gently loosen the skin of the turkey breast without completely detaching it. Spread a generous amount of the lemony butter mixture under the skin and over the top.
3. Roasting Tin Ready: Preheat your oven to 375°F (190°C). Place the butter-slathered turkey breast in the roasting tin.
4. Cook to Perfection: Roast the turkey breast in the oven for about 40-45 minutes, or until the internal temperature reads 165°F (74°C). The skin should be golden and crispy.
5. Rest & Slice: Once cooked, remove the turkey from the oven and allow it to rest for 10-15 minutes. This ensures the juices redistribute, keeping the meat tender. Slice and serve.

 ## ALTERNATIVE

- Herb Boost: Add finely chopped rosemary or thyme to the butter mixture for added depth of flavor.
- Spicy Kick: Introduce a bit of heat by adding a pinch of chili flakes or cayenne pepper to the butter.
- Citrus Variety: Substitute lemon with orange or lime for a different citrus note, adjusting the quantity based on the fruit's size and juice yield.

SLOW-COOKED BBQ PULLED PORK

Dive into the soul of Southern cooking with this slow-cooked BBQ pulled pork. Succulent pork shoulder, drenched in a rich and tangy barbecue sauce, becomes irresistibly tender and flavorful when adapted for the roasting tin.

 ## INGREDIENTS

- 500g pork shoulder
- Salt and black pepper, to taste
- 1/2 cup BBQ sauce, plus extra for serving
- 1/4 cup water or chicken broth
- 2 cloves garlic, minced
- 1 small onion, finely sliced
- 1 tsp smoked paprika or chipotle powder for added heat (optional)

 ## STEPS

1. Pork Prep: Preheat your oven to 300°F (150°C). Season the pork shoulder generously with salt and pepper. Place it in the roasting tin.
2. Sauce Mix: In a bowl, mix together the BBQ sauce, water or broth, minced garlic, and onion slices. Pour this mixture over the pork.
3. Low and Slow: Cover the roasting tin with aluminum foil and place it in the oven. Slow-cook for about 3-4 hours, or until the pork is tender and can be easily shredded with a fork.
4. Shred and Serve: Remove the roasting tin from the oven and shred the pork using two forks, mixing it well with the sauce. If desired, drizzle additional BBQ sauce over the top.
5. Optional Crisp: For added texture, you can place the uncovered roasting tin under a broiler for 2-3 minutes until the pork gets a slight crispy crust on top.

ALTERNATIVE

- Spice Mix-In: For a spicier kick, mix some chili powder or cayenne pepper into the BBQ sauce.
- Sweeter Variation: Add a touch of brown sugar or honey to the sauce for a sweeter profile.
- Veggie Additions: Include bell peppers or jalapeños in the sauce mix for added flavor and texture.

MUSTARD AND BROWN SUGAR PORK TENDERLOIN

Indulge in the harmonious blend of tangy mustard and sweet brown sugar, perfectly complementing the succulent pork tenderloin. Adapted for the roasting tin, this dish promises a caramelized exterior and juicy interior, making every bite a sweet and savory delight.

 ## INGREDIENTS

- 500g pork tenderloin
- 2 tbsp Dijon mustard
- 2 tbsp brown sugar
- Salt and black pepper, to taste
- 2 cloves garlic, minced
- 1 tbsp olive oil or melted butter
- 1 tsp rosemary, finely chopped (optional)
- 1/4 cup chicken broth or white wine

 ## STEPS

1. Pork Marination: Preheat your oven to 375°F (190°C). In a bowl, mix together the Dijon mustard, brown sugar, minced garlic, olive oil or butter, rosemary (if using), salt, and pepper. Coat the pork tenderloin evenly with this mixture and let it marinate for at least 20 minutes.
2. Roasting Tin Setup: Place the marinated pork tenderloin in the center of the roasting tin. Pour the chicken broth or white wine around the pork, ensuring it doesn't wash off the marinade.
3. Roast and Rest: Cover the roasting tin with aluminum foil and roast in the oven for about 25-30 minutes, or until the internal temperature of the pork reaches 145°F (63°C). Once done, let it rest for 5 minutes before slicing.
4. Serve and Savor: Slice the pork tenderloin into medallions and serve with your choice of sides. Drizzle with the pan juices for added flavor.

ALTERNATIVE

- Herb Enhancement: Mix in thyme or sage with the marinade for an added layer of flavor.
- Spicy Kick: Introduce a bit of cayenne pepper or chili flakes into the mustard mix for a spicy touch.
- Citrus Twist: Add a teaspoon of lemon or orange zest to the marinade for a fresh, citrusy hint.

ROASTED DUCK WITH ORANGE GLAZE

Experience a classic culinary combination with this roasted duck, enriched with a tangy and sweet orange glaze. Adapted for the roasting tin, this dish showcases a crispy skin and tender meat, elevated by the vibrant citrus notes from the glaze.

 ## INGREDIENTS

- 1 duck breast (about 400g)
- Salt and black pepper, to taste
- 2 tbsp olive oil or duck fat
- 1/2 cup fresh orange juice
- 2 tbsp honey or maple syrup
- 1 tbsp soy sauce
- 1 tsp fresh ginger, grated
- 1 garlic clove, minced
- 1 tsp orange zest
- 1/2 tsp dried thyme or rosemary (optional)

 ## STEPS

1. Duck Prep: Preheat your oven to 400°F (200°C). Score the duck skin in a crisscross pattern, season with salt and pepper.
2. Orange Glaze: Mix orange juice, honey/maple syrup, soy sauce, ginger, garlic, orange zest, and thyme/rosemary (optional).
3. Roasting Setup: Place duck breast, skin-side up, in a roasting tin. Drizzle with oil/duck fat. Pour half the glaze over the duck, ensuring skin coverage.
4. Roast & Glaze: Roast for 20 minutes. At the halfway mark, baste with the remaining glaze. Roast until crispy skin and desired doneness.
5. Rest & Serve: Rest for 5-7 minutes, slice, and serve with extra glaze and sides.

 ## ALTERNATIVE

- Spice It Up: Add a pinch of red chili flakes or a dash of sriracha to the glaze for a bit of heat.
- Citrus Variations: Experiment with different citrus like lemon or grapefruit in place of orange for a varied flavor profile.
- Herb Infusion: Marinate the duck with fresh herbs like basil or mint for an aromatic twist.

TERIYAKI BEEF ROAST

Dive into the rich flavors of East Asia with this Teriyaki Beef Roast. The roasting tin method ensures a succulent, tender beef infused with the sweet and savory teriyaki glaze, making it a delightful centerpiece for any meal.

 ## INGREDIENTS

- 400g beef roast (such as sirloin or rump)
- Salt and pepper, to taste
- 1/4 cup soy sauce
- 2 tbsp mirin
- 2 tbsp sake or white wine
- 2 tbsp brown sugar or honey
- 1 clove garlic, minced
- 1 tsp ginger, grated
- 1 tbsp olive or sesame oil
- 1 tbsp cornstarch mixed with 2 tbsp water (optional, for thicker glaze)
- Sliced green onions and sesame seeds, for garnish

 ## STEPS

1. Marinate: Whisk soy sauce, mirin, sake/white wine, brown sugar/honey, garlic, and ginger for the teriyaki marinade. Coat beef roast and marinate for 30 mins to 2 hours.
2. Oven Prep: Preheat the oven to 375°F (190°C). Place marinated beef in a roasting tin. Drizzle with olive/sesame oil, season with salt and pepper.
3. Roast: Roast for 25-30 mins or to your preferred doneness. Baste with reserved marinade halfway.
4. Make Glaze: Simmer reserved marinade in a saucepan until slightly reduced. For a thicker glaze, whisk in cornstarch-water mixture and cook until thickened.
5. Serve: Rest beef for 5-7 mins, slice, and drizzle with teriyaki glaze. Garnish with green onions and sesame seeds.

ALTERNATIVE

- Vegetable Boost: Roast some sliced bell peppers, onions, or broccoli in the roasting tin alongside the beef for added nutrition and flavor.
- Heat Kick: Add a dash of chili oil or some red pepper flakes to the marinade for a touch of spice.
- Sweet Variation: For a sweeter teriyaki glaze, add a splash of pineapple juice to the marinade.

GARLIC LEMON BUTTER SHRIMP ROAST

Indulge in the perfect symphony of zesty lemon, aromatic garlic, and succulent shrimp in this delightful roast. By utilizing the roasting tin, the shrimp are cooked to perfection, absorbing all the flavors while ensuring a delightful texture.

 ## INGREDIENTS

- 300g large shrimp, peeled and deveined
- 4 cloves garlic, minced
- Zest and juice of 1 lemon
- 4 tbsp unsalted butter, melted
- Salt and pepper, to taste
- 1 tbsp fresh parsley, finely chopped
- 1/2 tsp red pepper flakes (optional)
- Lemon wedges, for serving

 ## STEPS

1. Marinate: In a bowl, combine the melted butter, minced garlic, lemon zest, lemon juice, salt, pepper, and red pepper flakes (if using). Toss the shrimp in the mixture, ensuring they're well-coated.
2. Roasting Tin Preparation: Preheat your oven to 400°F (200°C). Arrange the marinated shrimp in a single layer within the roasting tin.
3. Roast: Place the tin in the oven and roast the shrimp for 8-10 minutes, or until they turn pink and are cooked through. Make sure not to overcook.
4. Serve: Remove the shrimp from the oven and sprinkle with fresh parsley. Give them a gentle toss to mix, then transfer to serving plates. Serve immediately with lemon wedges on the side.

 ## ALTERNATIVE

- Herb Twist: Try adding chopped dill or chives to the butter mixture for a different herbaceous note.
- Zesty Variation: Incorporate orange or lime zest and juice in place of or in addition to the lemon for a multi-citrus flavor.
- Cheese Touch: Sprinkle some grated Parmesan over the shrimp during the last 2 minutes of roasting for a cheesy finish.

HERB-CRUSTED SALMON FILLETS

Dive into the rich flavors of the sea with these herb-crusted salmon filets. The delicate texture of salmon paired with a crispy herb crust offers a harmonious blend of tastes and textures. This roasting tin method keeps the salmon moist while ensuring a golden crust.

 ## INGREDIENTS

- 2 salmon filets, skin on (about 150g each)
- 2 tbsp fresh parsley, finely chopped
- 1 tbsp fresh dill, finely chopped
- 1 tbsp fresh chives, finely chopped
- 2 cloves garlic, minced
- Zest of 1 lemon
- 2 tbsp breadcrumbs
- 2 tbsp olive oil
- Salt and pepper, to taste
- Lemon wedges, for serving

 ## STEPS

1. Herb Mixture: In a bowl, combine parsley, dill, chives, garlic, lemon zest, breadcrumbs, olive oil, salt, and pepper. Mix until it forms a paste-like consistency.
2. Prepare the Salmon: Preheat your oven to 400°F (200°C). Lay the salmon filets, skin-side down, in the roasting tin.
3. Apply Herb Crust: Evenly spread the herb mixture over the top of each salmon filet, pressing gently to adhere.
4. Roast: Place the roasting tin in the oven and roast for 12-15 minutes, or until the salmon easily flakes with a fork and the herb crust is golden.
5. Serve: Remove from the oven and transfer the salmon filets to plates. Serve with lemon wedges on the side.

ALTERNATIVE

- Different Herbs: Experiment with other herbs such as tarragon, basil, or cilantro for a different flavor profile.
- Nutty Twist: Add finely chopped almonds or pecans to the breadcrumb mixture for added crunch and nuttiness.
- Cheese Infusion: Introduce grated Parmesan or Pecorino Romano cheese to the herb mixture for a richer taste.

MEDITERRANEAN-STYLE ROASTED SEA BASS

Take a culinary journey to the Mediterranean coast with this delightful sea bass recipe. Infused with the aromatic flavors of olives, capers, and sun-dried tomatoes, this dish captures the essence of Mediterranean cuisine. Simplified using a roasting tin, it's a gourmet meal made easy.

 ## INGREDIENTS

- 2 sea bass fillets (about 150g each)
- 10 cherry tomatoes, halved
- 10 black or green olives, pitted and sliced
- 2 tbsp capers, drained
- 2 tbsp sun-dried tomatoes, thinly sliced
- 2 cloves garlic, minced
- Zest and juice of 1 lemon
- 2 tbsp olive oil
- 1 tbsp fresh parsley, finely chopped
- Salt and pepper, to taste

 ## STEPS

1. Sea Bass Prep: Preheat your oven to 400°F (200°C). Place the sea bass fillets, skin-side down, in the roasting tin.
2. Mediterranean Mixture: In a bowl, mix together the cherry tomatoes, olives, capers, sun-dried tomatoes, garlic, lemon zest, and half the lemon juice. Drizzle in the olive oil, season with salt and pepper, and toss until well combined.
3. Top the Sea Bass: Evenly distribute the Mediterranean mixture over the sea bass fillets.
4. Roast: Place the roasting tin in the oven and roast for 12-15 minutes, or until the sea bass is cooked through and flakes easily with a fork.
5. Garnish and Serve: Once out of the oven, sprinkle with fresh parsley and drizzle with the remaining lemon juice. Serve immediately.

ALTERNATIVE

- Herb Infusion: Add fresh basil or oregano for a deeper Mediterranean flavor.
- Citrus Twist: Use orange or lime zest/juice for a varied citrus note.
- Heat It Up: Add a sprinkle of red pepper flakes to the mixture for a subtle kick.

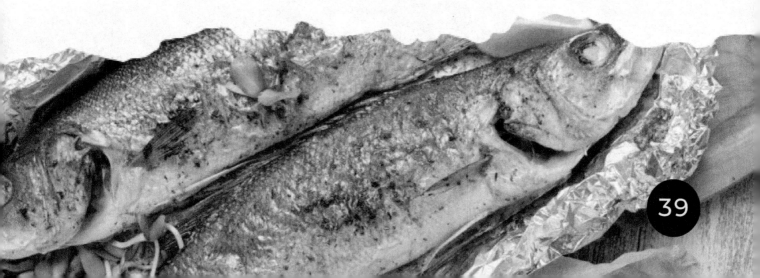

SPICY CAJUN CATFISH

Transport your tastebuds to the heart of Louisiana with this Spicy Cajun Catfish. Coated in a robust blend of seasonings, the catfish brings a kick of flavor, evoking the vibrant spirit of Cajun cuisine. Made effortlessly in a roasting tin, it's a bold dish that's surprisingly simple.

INGREDIENTS

- 2 catfish fillets (about 150g each)
- 2 tbsp olive oil
- 1 tbsp paprika
- 1 tsp dried thyme
- 1 tsp dried oregano
- 1/2 tsp cayenne pepper
- 1/2 tsp garlic powder
- 1/2 tsp onion powder
- 1/4 tsp black pepper
- Salt, to taste
- Lemon wedges, for serving

STEPS

1. Cajun Coating: Preheat your oven to 400°F (200°C). In a small bowl, mix together paprika, thyme, oregano, cayenne pepper, garlic powder, onion powder, black pepper, and salt.
2. Prepare Catfish: Rub the catfish fillets with olive oil, then coat them generously with the Cajun seasoning mixture on both sides.
3. Roast: Place the seasoned catfish fillets in the roasting tin and roast for 12-15 minutes, or until the fish is opaque and flakes easily with a fork.
4. Serve: Remove from the oven, and serve hot with lemon wedges on the side.

⬆ ALTERNATIVE

- Buttery Finish: Drizzle melted butter over the catfish just before serving for added richness.
- Green Topping: Sprinkle with freshly chopped parsley or cilantro for a fresh contrast.
- Dip on the Side: Serve with a cooling yogurt-based dip to balance out the heat.

TANGY CITRUS MAHI MAHI ROAST

Experience a burst of zesty flavors with this Tangy Citrus Mahi Mahi Roast. The combination of tangy citrus marinade with the meaty texture of Mahi Mahi creates a refreshing and flavorful dish. Perfectly suited for the roasting tin, this recipe offers an easy yet elegant dish for any occasion.

 ## INGREDIENTS

- 2 Mahi Mahi fillets (about 150g each)
- 2 tbsp olive oil
- Zest and juice of 1 lemon
- Zest and juice of 1 orange
- 2 garlic cloves, minced
- 1 tsp honey or agave syrup
- 1/4 tsp red pepper flakes (adjust to taste)
- Salt and black pepper, to taste
- Fresh cilantro or parsley, for garnish

 ## STEPS

1. Citrus Marinade: In a bowl, whisk together olive oil, lemon zest, lemon juice, orange zest, orange juice, minced garlic, honey, red pepper flakes, salt, and black pepper.
2. Marinate Mahi Mahi: Place the Mahi Mahi fillets in the roasting tin and pour the marinade over them. Ensure the fillets are well-coated. Let them marinate for about 20 minutes.
3. Roast: Preheat your oven to 400°F (200°C). Transfer the roasting tin with the marinated Mahi Mahi to the oven and roast for 12-15 minutes, or until the fish is opaque and flakes easily with a fork.
4. Serve: Once roasted, transfer the Mahi Mahi to plates, drizzle with any remaining sauce from the tin, and garnish with fresh cilantro or parsley.

ALTERNATIVE

- Tropical Twist: Top the roasted Mahi Mahi with a mango salsa for a sweet contrast.
- Heat Level: Add chopped jalapeños to the marinade for an extra kick.
- Herb Infusion: Mix in some chopped fresh mint to the marinade for a refreshing twist.

GARLIC PARMESAN ROASTED SCALLOPS

Elevate your seafood game with these Garlic Parmesan Roasted Scallops. The rich, buttery flavor of scallops combined with garlic and a hint of Parmesan cheese is an indulgence that's surprisingly easy to prepare. Using a roasting tin streamlines the process, allowing the flavors to meld beautifully.

 ## INGREDIENTS

- 12 large scallops (approximately 250g)
- 2 tbsp olive oil
- 3 garlic cloves, minced
- 1/4 cup grated Parmesan cheese
- 2 tbsp fresh parsley, finely chopped
- 1 tbsp unsalted butter, melted
- Salt and black pepper, to taste
- Lemon wedges, for serving

 ## STEPS

1. Preparation: Pat scallops dry with a paper towel. Remove the side muscle if attached.
2. Scallop Mixture: In a bowl, combine the olive oil, minced garlic, grated Parmesan, melted butter, chopped parsley, salt, and black pepper. Gently mix in the scallops until they are well-coated with the mixture.
3. Roast: Preheat your oven to 425°F (220°C). Arrange the scallops in a single layer in the roasting tin. Transfer to the oven and roast for 10-12 minutes or until scallops are opaque and have a golden crust.
4. Serve: Once done, plate the scallops and drizzle any sauce left in the roasting tin over them. Serve with lemon wedges on the side.

ALTERNATIVE

- Herb Variations: Replace parsley with fresh basil or dill for a different flavor profile.
- Add Heat: Mix in a pinch of red pepper flakes or cayenne to the scallop mixture for a spicy kick.
- Breaded Delight: For added texture, sprinkle some panko breadcrumbs on top before roasting.

BLACKENED TILAPIA WITH LIME BUTTER

Discover the vibrant flavors of blackened tilapia, enhanced with a zesty lime butter. This dish captures a bold spice blend that beautifully complements the mild taste of tilapia. Using a roasting tin ensures even cooking and absorption of flavors.

 ## INGREDIENTS

- 2 tilapia fillets (approximately 300g total)
- 1 tbsp olive oil
- 1 tsp smoked paprika
- 1 tsp onion powder
- 1 tsp garlic powder
- 1/2 tsp cayenne pepper
- 1/2 tsp dried thyme
- 1/2 tsp dried oregano
- Salt and black pepper, to taste
- For the Lime Butter:
- 2 tbsp unsalted butter, softened
- Zest of 1 lime
- 1 tbsp lime juice
- A pinch of salt

 ## STEPS

1. Preparation: Mix the smoked paprika, onion powder, garlic powder, cayenne pepper, dried thyme, dried oregano, salt, and black pepper in a bowl to create the blackening spice.
2. Tilapia Seasoning: Brush the tilapia fillets with olive oil and then generously coat both sides with the blackening spice mixture.
3. Roast: Preheat your oven to 425°F (220°C). Place the seasoned tilapia fillets in the roasting tin. Transfer to the oven and roast for 12-15 minutes or until the fish flakes easily with a fork.
4. Lime Butter Preparation: While the tilapia is roasting, mix the softened butter with lime zest, lime juice, and a pinch of salt.
5. Serve: Once the tilapia is done roasting, plate the fillets and dollop the lime butter over the hot fish, allowing it to melt and infuse the fish with flavor.

ALTERNATIVE

- Herb Infusion: Add finely chopped cilantro or parsley to the lime butter for an herbal twist.
- Zesty Option: Replace lime with lemon or orange for a different citrus flavor.
- Add Veggies: Consider adding sliced bell peppers and onions to the roasting tin for a fuller meal. Adjust roasting time as needed.

SWEET CHILI GLAZED COD

Immerse yourself in the delightful combination of sweet and spicy with this sweet chili glazed cod. The tender flakiness of the cod pairs flawlessly with a glossy, sticky glaze, making it a delightful main for any meal. Adapted for the roasting tin, you'll find this dish not only flavorful but also effortlessly easy.

 ## INGREDIENTS

- 2 cod fillets (approximately 300g total)
- 1 tbsp olive oil
- Salt and pepper, to taste

For the Sweet Chili Glaze:
- 3 tbsp sweet chili sauce
- 1 tbsp soy sauce
- 1 tbsp honey or maple syrup
- 1 tsp fresh ginger, grated
- 1 clove garlic, minced
- Zest and juice of half a lime

 ## STEPS

1. Glaze Preparation: In a bowl, whisk together sweet chili sauce, soy sauce, honey or maple syrup, grated ginger, minced garlic, lime zest, and lime juice until well combined.
2. Cod Preparation: Lightly brush the cod fillets with olive oil, and season with salt and pepper.
3. Apply Glaze: Generously brush the cod fillets with the sweet chili glaze, ensuring they're well-coated.
4. Roast: Preheat your oven to 400°F (200°C). Place the glazed cod fillets in the roasting tin. Transfer to the oven and roast for 12-15 minutes, or until the cod is opaque and flakes easily with a fork.
5. Serve: Once cooked, remove the cod from the oven. Drizzle with any remaining glaze from the roasting tin and serve immediately.

ALTERNATIVE

- Heat Boost: Add a dash of sriracha or diced red chili to the glaze for extra heat.
- Citrus Burst: Consider replacing lime with lemon or orange for a varied citrus note.
- Side Pairing: Serve the cod on a bed of steamed jasmine rice or roasted vegetables for a complete meal.

PESTO-STUFFED RAINBOW TROUT

Step into a burst of Italian-inspired flavors with this pesto-stuffed rainbow trout. The rich and aromatic pesto complements the trout's delicate flesh, resulting in a symphony of flavors with every bite. Adapted for the roasting tin, this dish is a testament to simplicity yielding incredible results.

 ## INGREDIENTS

 ## STEPS

- 2 rainbow trout fillets (approximately 400g total)
- 4 tbsp pesto (store-bought or homemade)
- 1 tbsp olive oil
- Salt and pepper, to taste
- Lemon wedges and fresh basil leaves, for garnish

1. Preparation: Preheat your oven to 400°F (200°C). Clean and pat dry the trout fillets. Season the inside and outside of each trout with salt and pepper.
2. Stuff with Pesto: Gently spread about 2 tablespoons of pesto inside each trout.
3. Arrange in Roasting Tin: Drizzle a roasting tin with olive oil. Place the stuffed trout fillets in the roasting tin.
4. Roast: Transfer the roasting tin to the preheated oven and roast the trout for 15-20 minutes, or until the flesh is opaque and flakes easily.
5. Serve: Once roasted, remove from the oven and plate the trout. Garnish with fresh basil leaves and serve with lemon wedges on the side.

 ## ALTERNATIVE

- Homemade Pesto: If you opt for homemade pesto, consider experimenting with nuts like almonds or walnuts instead of traditional pine nuts.
- Veggie Boost: Add finely sliced sun-dried tomatoes or spinach inside the trout along with the pesto for added texture and flavor.
- Crunch Factor: For a crispy finish, consider adding a breadcrumb topping or sliced almonds on top of the trout before roasting.

BAKED CLAMS OREGANATA

Unearth the flavors of the sea with these baked clams oreganata. Clams are topped with a delightful mixture of breadcrumbs, garlic, and oregano, then roasted to perfection. Adapted for the roasting tin, this dish promises a tantalizing taste of the ocean with a crispy, golden crust.

 ## INGREDIENTS

- 12 fresh littleneck clams, scrubbed
- 1/2 cup breadcrumbs
- 2 tbsp fresh oregano, finely chopped (or 2 tsp dried oregano)
- 2 cloves garlic, minced
- 2 tbsp grated Parmesan cheese
- 2 tbsp olive oil
- 1/4 tsp red pepper flakes (optional)
- Salt and pepper, to taste
- Lemon wedges and fresh parsley, for garnish

 ## STEPS

1. Prep the Clams: Shuck the clams, discarding the top shell. Arrange the clams on their half shells in the roasting tin.
2. Breadcrumb Mixture: In a bowl, combine breadcrumbs, oregano, garlic, Parmesan, red pepper flakes (if using), olive oil, salt, and pepper. Mix well until the breadcrumbs are evenly coated with the oil.
3. Top the Clams: Carefully spoon the breadcrumb mixture onto each clam, pressing lightly to ensure the topping adheres.
4. Roast: Preheat your oven to 425°F (220°C). Transfer the roasting tin to the oven and bake for 10-12 minutes, or until the breadcrumbs are golden brown and crispy.
5. Serve: Remove the clams from the oven and transfer them to serving plates. Garnish with fresh parsley and serve with lemon wedges on the side.

ALTERNATIVE

- Herb Variation: If oregano isn't to your liking, try using fresh basil or thyme for a different herbaceous note.
- Cheese Choice: Swap out Parmesan for pecorino or Asiago for a variation in cheesy flavor.
- Zesty Touch: Zest some lemon into the breadcrumb mixture for an added citrusy punch.

SPINACH AND FETA FRITTATA

Start your day with a delightful blend of breakfast favorites baked together in this Sausage, Egg, and Cheese Casserole. Perfectly seasoned sausage crumbles, fluffy eggs, and melted cheese combine in the roasting tin for a dish that's both hearty and delicious.

 ## INGREDIENTS

- 2 fresh breakfast sausages, casings removed
- 4 large eggs, beaten
- 1/2 cup cheddar cheese, shredded
- 1/4 cup milk
- 1/4 cup green bell pepper, diced
- 1/4 cup red onion, finely chopped
- 1/4 tsp paprika
- Salt and pepper, to taste
- Fresh parsley or chives, for garnish

 ## STEPS

1. Brown the Sausage: In a skillet over medium heat, crumble and cook the sausage until browned and no longer pink. Remove from heat and drain excess fat.
2. Casserole Mixture: In a mixing bowl, combine the cooked sausage, beaten eggs, milk, bell pepper, onion, paprika, salt, and pepper. Mix until well combined.
3. Assemble in Roasting Tin: Pour the mixture into the roasting tin and sprinkle the shredded cheddar cheese evenly over the top.
4. Roast: Preheat your oven to 375°F (190°C). Transfer the roasting tin to the oven and bake for 20-25 minutes, or until the eggs are set and the top is golden brown.
5. Serve: Remove from the oven and let it cool slightly. Garnish with fresh parsley or chives before serving.

ALTERNATIVE

- Meat Variation: Swap out sausage for diced bacon or ham for a different meaty flavor.
- Vegetable Boost: Add in vegetables like spinach, mushrooms, or cherry tomatoes for added nutrition and flavor.
- Cheese Choice: Replace cheddar with mozzarella, feta, or pepper jack for a variation in cheesy delight.

ROASTED VEGGIE AND HAM QUICHE

Step into a comforting world of savory delight with this Roasted Veggie and Ham Quiche. A harmony of roasted vegetables, succulent ham, and creamy custard filling makes this dish a timeless favorite. Simplified for the roasting tin, breakfast or brunch is now easier than ever.

 ## INGREDIENTS

 ## STEPS

- 1 pre-made pie crust (optional)
- 4 large eggs
- 1/4 cup heavy cream or milk
- 1/2 cup diced ham
- 1/2 cup mixed roasted vegetables (e.g. bell peppers, zucchini, cherry tomatoes)
- 1/4 cup grated cheddar or Gruyère cheese
- 2 tbsp fresh chives, chopped
- Salt and pepper, to taste
- Olive oil, for drizzling

1. Prep Crust (If Using): If using a pie crust, lay it into the roasting tin and press it into the edges. Prick the base with a fork.
2. Mix Ingredients: In a mixing bowl, combine the eggs, heavy cream or milk, salt, and pepper. Whisk until well combined. Stir in the roasted vegetables, diced ham, and cheese.
3. Assemble in Roasting Tin: Pour the egg mixture over the crust, ensuring the ingredients are evenly distributed.
4. Roast: Preheat your oven to 375°F (190°C). Place the roasting tin in the oven and bake for 20-25 minutes, or until the quiche is set in the center and lightly golden.
5. Serve: Remove from the oven and sprinkle with fresh chives. Let it cool slightly before slicing and serving.

 ## ALTERNATIVE

- Crustless Option: For a lighter, gluten-free variation, simply omit the pie crust.
- Cheese Varieties: Experiment with other cheeses such as feta, mozzarella, or blue cheese for a distinct flavor.
- Go Vegetarian: Omit the ham and double up on the veggies or add sautéed mushrooms for a vegetarian version.

BREAKFAST HASH WITH SUNNY SIDE UP EGGS

Dive into a delightful morning feast with this Breakfast Hash crowned with Sunny Side Up Eggs. A medley of diced potatoes, aromatic vegetables, and flavorful spices serves as the base, while perfectly cooked eggs provide a creamy contrast. Tailored for the roasting tin, this dish ensures a hassle-free breakfast experience.

 ## INGREDIENTS

- 2 large eggs
- 2 medium-sized potatoes, diced into small cubes
- 1/2 bell pepper, diced
- 1/4 cup diced red onion
- 1/4 cup diced cooked bacon or sausage (optional)
- 1 clove garlic, minced
- 1 tsp smoked paprika
- 1 tsp dried rosemary or thyme (or a mix of both)
- 2 tbsp olive oil
- Salt and pepper, to taste
- Fresh chives or parsley, for garnish

 ## STEPS

1. Roasting Tin Prep: Preheat your oven to 400°F (200°C). In a mixing bowl, combine the diced potatoes, bell pepper, onion, garlic, smoked paprika, rosemary or thyme, and olive oil. Toss until everything is well coated.
2. Roast the Hash: Transfer the vegetable mix to the roasting tin, spreading it out in an even layer. If adding bacon or sausage, sprinkle them over the top. Roast for 20-25 minutes, stirring halfway through, until the potatoes are golden and almost done.
3. Add the Eggs: Make two small wells in the hash using a spoon. Crack an egg into each well, being careful not to break the yolk.
4. Final Roasting: Return the roasting tin to the oven and bake for an additional 6-8 minutes, or until the egg whites are set but yolks remain runny.
5. Serve: Season with additional salt and pepper if needed. Garnish with fresh chives or parsley. Serve directly from the roasting tin or plate individually.

ALTERNATIVE

- Go Meatless: For a vegetarian version, omit the bacon/sausage and add veggies like zucchini, mushroom, or spinach.
- Cheesy Delight: Add grated cheddar or pepper jack cheese over the hash before adding the eggs for a cheesy twist.
- Spice It Up: For those who enjoy a kick, sprinkle some red chili flakes or drizzle hot sauce over the finished dish.

BLUEBERRY ALMOND BAKED OATMEAL

Indulge in the sweet harmony of juicy blueberries and crunchy almonds with this Blueberry Almond Baked Oatmeal. A delightful fusion of wholesome oats, creamy almond butter, and fragrant vanilla, this dish turns a simple breakfast into an irresistible treat. Crafted for the roasting tin, this baked oatmeal is easy to prepare and even easier to enjoy.

 ## INGREDIENTS

- 1 cup old-fashioned rolled oats
- 1/2 cup fresh or frozen blueberries
- 1/4 cup almond slices or chopped almonds
- 2 tbsp almond butter
- 1 1/2 cups almond milk (or milk of choice)
- 2 tbsp maple syrup or honey
- 1 tsp vanilla extract
- 1/2 tsp ground cinnamon
- 1/4 tsp salt
- Optional toppings: additional blueberries, almond slices, a drizzle of almond butter, or yogurt

 ## STEPS

1. Roasting Tin Prep: Preheat your oven to 375°F (190°C). Lightly grease your roasting tin with a bit of almond butter or cooking spray.
2. Mix Ingredients: In a large mixing bowl, combine the rolled oats, blueberries, almond slices, almond butter, almond milk, maple syrup, vanilla extract, cinnamon, and salt. Stir until well combined.
3. Transfer & Bake: Pour the mixture into the prepared roasting tin, ensuring it's spread evenly. If using fresh blueberries, you can press a few more into the top for added aesthetics.
4. Baking: Place the roasting tin in the oven and bake for 25-30 minutes, or until the edges start to turn golden and the center is set.
5. Cool & Serve: Remove from the oven and let it cool slightly. Slice and serve warm. If desired, top with additional blueberries, almond slices, a drizzle of almond butter, or a dollop of yogurt.

ALTERNATIVE

- Nut Swap: Replace almonds with walnuts, pecans, or any other favorite nut.
- Berry Mix: Instead of just blueberries, consider adding a mix of berries like raspberries, strawberries, or blackberries.
- Choco Twist: For a sweet variation, sprinkle in a handful of dark chocolate chips before baking

TOMATO, BASIL, AND MOZZARELLA STRATA

Elevate your morning with the timeless pairing of tomatoes, basil, and mozzarella in this hearty Strata. This dish elegantly combines crusty bread soaked in a rich egg mixture with the freshness of tomatoes and basil, crowned with the melt-in-mouth goodness of mozzarella. Expertly tailored for the roasting tin, it ensures both ease of preparation and a burst of Mediterranean flavors.

 ## INGREDIENTS

- 3 cups crusty bread, cubed
- 1 medium tomato, sliced
- 1/2 cup fresh mozzarella cheese, sliced or cubed
- 2 tbsp fresh basil leaves, chopped (plus extra for garnish)
- 4 large eggs
- 1 cup whole milk
- 1 garlic clove, minced
- 1/4 tsp salt
- 1/4 tsp black pepper
- 1/4 tsp red pepper flakes (optional)
- Olive oil or cooking spray, for greasing

 ## STEPS

1. Roasting Tin Prep: Preheat your oven to 375°F (190°C). Lightly grease your roasting tin with olive oil or cooking spray.
2. Layer Ingredients: In the roasting tin, layer half of the bread cubes. Top with half of the tomato slices, half of the mozzarella, and sprinkle with half of the chopped basil. Repeat the layering with the remaining ingredients.
3. Egg Mixture: In a mixing bowl, whisk together eggs, milk, minced garlic, salt, black pepper, and red pepper flakes (if using). Pour this mixture evenly over the layered ingredients in the roasting tin.
4. Bake: Place the roasting tin in the oven and bake for 25-30 minutes, or until the egg is set and the top is golden and crispy.
5. Serve: Remove from the oven, let it cool slightly, and garnish with additional fresh basil. Serve warm.

ALTERNATIVE

- Meaty Addition: For a non-vegetarian twist, add some cooked and crumbled bacon or pancetta between the layers.
- Cheese Variety: Swap out mozzarella for fontina, gouda, or any other melting cheese of your choice.
- Veggie Boost: Incorporate spinach, mushrooms, or bell peppers for added flavors and nutrition.

SWEET POTATO AND BACON BREAKFAST ROAST

Indulge in the harmonious blend of savory bacon and subtly sweet potatoes in this hearty breakfast roast. Perfect for a lazy morning or when you need a meal that delivers on flavor and satisfaction. Roasted to perfection in a tin, this dish guarantees a delightful crunch on the outside with a soft, flavorful inside.

INGREDIENTS

- 2 medium sweet potatoes, peeled and diced into 1-inch cubes
- 6 strips of bacon, cut into 1-inch pieces
- 1 small red onion, thinly sliced
- 2 cloves garlic, minced
- 2 tbsp olive oil
- 1/2 tsp smoked paprika
- 1/4 tsp ground cinnamon
- Salt and black pepper, to taste
- 2 large eggs (optional, for topping)
- Fresh chives or green onions, chopped, for garnish

STEPS

1. Roasting Tin Prep: Preheat your oven to 400°F (200°C). Lightly grease your roasting tin with olive oil or cooking spray.
2. Toss and Layer: In a large bowl, toss the diced sweet potatoes with olive oil, minced garlic, smoked paprika, cinnamon, salt, and pepper. Once well coated, spread them out evenly in the roasting tin. Scatter the bacon pieces and red onion slices over the sweet potatoes.
3. Roast: Place the tin in the oven and roast for 20-25 minutes, stirring halfway through, until sweet potatoes are tender and bacon is crispy.
4. Eggs (Optional): Make small wells in the roast, crack an egg into each well, and return to the oven. Roast for an additional 7-10 minutes, or until the egg whites are set and yolks remain runny.
5. Serve: Remove from the oven, season with additional salt and pepper if needed, and sprinkle with chopped chives or green onions. Serve immediately.

ALTERNATIVE

- Spice It Up: Add a sprinkle of chili flakes or cayenne pepper for an extra kick.
- Veggie Boost: Mix in bell peppers, cherry tomatoes, or spinach for added color and nutrition.
- Cheese Delight: Sprinkle some feta or cheddar cheese over the top 5 minutes before the end of the roasting time for a cheesy twist.

APPLE CINNAMON FRENCH TOAST BAKE

Dive into a comforting blend of soft, custardy bread combined with the warm flavors of cinnamon and apple in this delightful breakfast bake. By adapting this classic dish to a roasting tin, we ensure an even cooking process and a delightful crispy top layer, making your morning meal both delicious and hassle-free.

INGREDIENTS

- 4 slices day-old bread (like brioche or challah), cut into 1-inch cubes
- 1 medium apple, peeled, cored, and diced
- 2 large eggs
- 1 cup whole milk
- 3 tbsp maple syrup, plus extra for serving
- 1 tsp vanilla extract
- 1 tsp ground cinnamon
- 1/4 tsp ground nutmeg
- Pinch of salt
- Powdered sugar, for dusting (optional)
- 1 tbsp unsalted butter, diced into small pieces

STEPS

1. Roasting Tin Prep: Preheat your oven to 375°F (190°C). Lightly grease your roasting tin with butter or cooking spray.
2. Bread Layering: Evenly spread the bread cubes in the roasting tin. Scatter the diced apples over the bread.
3. Custard Mix: In a medium-sized bowl, whisk together the eggs, milk, maple syrup, vanilla extract, cinnamon, nutmeg, and a pinch of salt. Pour this mixture over the bread and apples, ensuring all the bread is soaked.
4. Top with Butter: Dot the top with small pieces of butter.
5. Bake: Transfer the roasting tin to the oven and bake for 25-30 minutes, or until the top is golden brown and the custard is set.
6. Serve: Once baked, remove from the oven and allow it to cool slightly. Dust with powdered sugar, drizzle with additional maple syrup, and serve warm.

ALTERNATIVE

- Berry Delight: Replace apples with a mix of berries like raspberries, blueberries, and blackberries for a berry-infused version.
- Creamy Indulgence: Add a dollop of whipped cream or a scoop of vanilla ice cream when serving.
- Nutty Twist: Scatter some chopped walnuts or pecans over the top before baking for added crunch and flavor.

MEDITERRANEAN BREAKFAST WRAPS

Embrace the vibrant flavors of the Mediterranean in the morning with these delectable breakfast wraps. Stuffed with a mix of sautéed vegetables, eggs, and feta, and baked to perfection in a roasting tin, these wraps offer a twist to your typical breakfast fare while still being hearty and fulfilling.

 ## INGREDIENTS

- 2 large tortilla wraps
- 4 large eggs, lightly beaten
- 1 small red bell pepper, finely diced
- 1 small zucchini, finely diced
- 1/2 small red onion, finely chopped
- 1/4 cup crumbled feta cheese
- 2 tbsp olive oil
- 1 tsp dried oregano
- Salt and pepper, to taste
- Fresh parsley, finely chopped for garnish
- 2 tbsp hummus, for serving (optional)

 ## STEPS

1. Vegetable Sauté: In a skillet over medium heat, warm the olive oil. Add the bell pepper, zucchini, and red onion. Sauté until the vegetables are soft and slightly caramelized, about 5-7 minutes.
2. Egg Addition: Pour the beaten eggs over the sautéed vegetables. Stir gently to combine, cooking until the eggs are just set but still slightly runny. Season with oregano, salt, and pepper. Remove from heat.
3. Wrap Assembly: Lay out the tortilla wraps on a flat surface. Divide the egg and vegetable mixture between the wraps, placing it slightly off-center. Sprinkle feta cheese over each portion. Carefully roll up each wrap, tucking in the sides as you go.
4. Roasting Tin Prep: Preheat your oven to 375°F (190°C) and lightly grease your roasting tin.
5. Bake: Place the assembled wraps seam-side down in the roasting tin. Bake for 10-12 minutes, or until the wraps are golden brown and slightly crispy.
6. Serve: Remove from the oven, slice each wrap in half, and garnish with fresh parsley. Serve with a dollop of hummus on the side, if desired.

 ## ALTERNATIVE

- Meaty Twist: Add some diced grilled chicken or slices of gyro meat for added protein.
- Spicy Kick: Introduce some thinly sliced chili peppers or a dash of hot sauce for some heat.
- Cheese Variety: Swap out feta for goat cheese or mozzarella for a different flavor profile.

ROASTED VEGETABLE RATATOUILLE

Dive into the rustic flavors of Provence with this Roasted Vegetable Ratatouille. A medley of colorful veggies slow-cooked to perfection, bringing out their natural sweetness and mingling their aromas for a comforting and aromatic dish.

 ## INGREDIENTS

- 1 medium zucchini, sliced
- 1 medium eggplant, diced
- 1 red bell pepper, deseeded and sliced
- 1 yellow bell pepper, deseeded and sliced
- 2 medium tomatoes, diced
- 1 red onion, sliced
- 2 cloves garlic, minced
- 3 tbsp olive oil
- 1 tsp dried thyme
- 1 tsp dried rosemary
- Salt and black pepper, to taste
- Fresh basil leaves for garnish

 ## STEPS

1. Preparation: Preheat your oven to 375°F (190°C).
2. Layer the Veggies: In a roasting tin, spread out the zucchini, eggplant, bell peppers, tomatoes, and red onion. Sprinkle the minced garlic over the vegetables.
3. Season: Drizzle with olive oil and evenly sprinkle thyme, rosemary, salt, and black pepper. Toss the vegetables to coat them in the seasoning.
4. Roast: Place the roasting tin in the oven and roast for about 25-30 minutes, stirring once or twice, until the vegetables are tender and have taken on a golden hue.
5. Serve: Dish out the ratatouille into bowls or plates. Garnish with fresh basil leaves.

 ## ALTERNATIVE

- Hearty Add-In: To make it a more substantial dish, add chickpeas or white beans before roasting.
- Cheese Topper: Before the final 10 minutes of roasting, sprinkle some crumbled feta or goat cheese on top for a creamy finish.
- Spice Kick: Add a pinch of red chili flakes for an extra zing.

MUSHROOM AND SPINACH LASAGNA

Dive into layers of earthy mushrooms, fresh spinach, and creamy béchamel, all harmoniously layered between sheets of pasta. This Mushroom and Spinach Lasagna is a vegetarian feast crafted specifically for the roasting tin.

 ## INGREDIENTS

- 4 lasagna sheets
- 200g fresh mushrooms, thinly sliced
- 100g fresh spinach, washed
- 2 cloves garlic, minced
- 150ml béchamel sauce (store-bought or homemade)
- 100g grated mozzarella cheese
- 2 tbsp olive oil
- Salt and black pepper, to taste
- Grated Parmesan and fresh basil leaves for garnish

STEPS

1. Roasting Tin Prep: Preheat oven to 375°F (190°C). Oil tin.
2. Mushroom & Spinach Layer: Spread mushrooms, spinach, garlic, salt, pepper.
3. Lasagna Layering: Fit sheets, add half béchamel, half mozzarella.
4. Repeat: More mushrooms, spinach, sheets, béchamel, mozzarella.
5. Roast: Cover with foil, bake 25-30 mins until tender, golden.

Serve: Rest 10 mins, top with Parmesan, basil. Enjoy! (450 characters)

ALTERNATIVE

- Extra Veggies: Incorporate thinly sliced bell peppers or zucchini for added nutrition and flavor.
- Cheese Variation: Add some ricotta or feta cheese layers for a different cheesy profile.
- Spice It Up: A pinch of red pepper flakes in the mushroom and spinach mixture can elevate the heat factor.

SPAGHETTI SQUASH PRIMAVERA

Unearth the wonders of spaghetti squash as it takes center stage in this vibrant, vegetable-loaded dish. Designed exclusively for the roasting tin, this twist on the classic primavera is both light and gratifying.

 ## INGREDIENTS

- 1 medium-sized spaghetti squash (around 500g), halved lengthwise and seeds removed
- 100g cherry tomatoes, halved
- 50g bell peppers (a mix of colors), thinly sliced
- 50g asparagus tips
- 50g broccoli florets, cut into small pieces
- 1 clove garlic, minced
- 2 tbsp olive oil
- Salt and black pepper, to taste
- Grated Parmesan and fresh basil or parsley for garnish
- 1 tbsp lemon juice
- Zest of half a lemon

 ## STEPS

1. Roasting Tin Prep: Preheat oven to 400°F (200°C). Drizzle 1 tbsp olive oil in tin.
2. Squash Prep: Halve squash, place cut side down in tin. Roast 30-35 mins until tender, fork-shreddable.
3. Veggie Toss: Mix tomatoes, peppers, asparagus, broccoli, garlic, remaining oil, lemon juice, zest, salt, pepper in a bowl.
4. Add Veggies: Flip squash, place veg mix around it. Roast 12-15 mins until tender and slightly charred.

Shred & Serve: Fork-shred squash, mix with veggies. Garnish with Parmesan and herbs. Enjoy!

 ## ALTERNATIVE

- Protein Boost: Add some grilled chicken strips or sautéed shrimp for an added protein punch.
- Cheesy Delight: Mix in some feta or goat cheese for a creamy, tangy flavor.
- Spice Factor: A sprinkle of crushed red pepper flakes can intensify the heat and give a zesty kick.

CHICKPEA AND VEGETABLE CURRY

Delight in the aromatic spices and textures in this hearty chickpea and vegetable curry. Effortlessly crafted in the roasting tin, this vegan-friendly dish brims with flavor, nutrition, and comfort.

 ## INGREDIENTS

- 1 can (400g) chickpeas, drained and rinsed
- 150g cauliflower florets
- 100g sweet potato, diced into 1-inch pieces
- 50g green peas (fresh or frozen)
- 1 medium onion, thinly sliced
- 2 cloves garlic, minced
- 1 inch ginger, minced
- 2 tbsp curry powder
- 1 tsp turmeric powder
- 1 tsp cumin seeds
- 200ml coconut milk
- 2 tbsp tomato paste
- 2 tbsp olive oil
- Salt, to taste
- Fresh coriander (cilantro) for garnish

 ## STEPS

1. Roasting Tin Preparation: Preheat your oven to 400°F (200°C). In the roasting tin, combine olive oil, garlic, ginger, curry powder, turmeric, cumin seeds, salt, and tomato paste. Mix well to form a paste.
2. Toss the Ingredients: Add chickpeas, cauliflower florets, sweet potatoes, green peas, and sliced onions to the roasting tin. Toss everything well to ensure they're evenly coated with the spice mixture.
3. Roast: Place the tin in the preheated oven and roast for about 20 minutes.
4. Add Coconut Milk: After 20 minutes, carefully remove the tin from the oven. Pour the coconut milk over the vegetables, stirring to mix it into the spices and veggies.
5. Continue to Roast: Return the tin to the oven for another 15-20 minutes, or until the vegetables are tender and the curry sauce has thickened slightly.
6. Garnish and Serve: Remove from the oven, and garnish with freshly chopped coriander (cilantro). Serve hot with rice, naan, or on its own.

 ## ALTERNATIVE

- Additional Protein: Stir in cubed tofu or paneer for an extra protein boost.
- Heat It Up: Add a finely chopped chili pepper or a dash of cayenne for a spicier kick.
- Variety of Vegetables: Feel free to use other vegetables like bell peppers, zucchini, or eggplant to mix things up.

STUFFED BELL PEPPERS

Revel in the delightful combination of tender bell peppers filled with a savory mixture of grains, vegetables, and seasonings. This classic dish, effortlessly adapted for the roasting tin, offers a wholesome meal that's as pleasing to the eyes as it is to the palate.

 ## INGREDIENTS

 ## STEPS

- 2 large bell peppers (any color), tops removed and seeds discarded
- 100g cooked quinoa or rice
- 50g canned black beans, drained and rinsed
- 50g sweet corn kernels (fresh or frozen)
- 50g diced tomatoes (fresh or canned)
- 1 small onion, finely chopped
- 2 cloves garlic, minced
- 50g shredded cheese (like cheddar or mozzarella; optional)
- 2 tbsp olive oil
- 1 tsp ground cumin
- 1 tsp smoked paprika
- Salt and black pepper, to taste
- Fresh parsley or cilantro, for garnish

1. Roasting Tin Preparation: Preheat your oven to 375°F (190°C). Brush the outer skin of the bell peppers with a little olive oil and set aside.
2. Prepare Filling: In a mixing bowl, combine cooked quinoa or rice, black beans, sweet corn, diced tomatoes, chopped onion, minced garlic, ground cumin, smoked paprika, half of the cheese (if using), olive oil, salt, and black pepper. Mix until well combined.
3. Stuff the Peppers: Fill each bell pepper with the quinoa mixture, pressing down gently to pack the filling.
4. Roast: Place the stuffed peppers in the roasting tin, ensuring they stand upright. Sprinkle the remaining cheese on top (if using).
5. Cover and Cook: Cover the roasting tin with aluminum foil and bake in the preheated oven for about 30-35 minutes or until the peppers are tender.
6. Serve: Once cooked, remove the peppers from the oven and let them cool slightly. Garnish with fresh parsley or cilantro. Serve warm.

ALTERNATIVE

- Meat Lovers: Add ground beef, turkey, or chicken to the mix for a meatier filling.
- Different Grains: Swap out quinoa or rice for farro, barley, or couscous.
- Vegan Cheese: Use plant-based cheese or nutritional yeast for a dairy-free version.

ASPARAGUS TART

Indulge in the bright, earthy flavors of asparagus showcased on a flaky pastry base. Adapting this classic springtime favorite for the roasting tin not only simplifies the process but also results in a beautifully presented dish that's perfect for any meal or occasion.

 ## INGREDIENTS

- 1 sheet puff pastry (thawed if frozen), cut to fit the roasting tin
- 100g fresh asparagus spears, tough ends trimmed
- 100g ricotta cheese or cream cheese, softened
- 1 garlic clove, minced
- Zest of 1 lemon
- 1 tbsp olive oil
- Salt and black pepper, to taste
- Grated Parmesan cheese, for topping (optional)
- Fresh herbs such as dill or chives, for garnish

 ## STEPS

1. Roasting Tin Preparation: Preheat your oven to 400°F (200°C). Lightly grease the roasting tin or line it with parchment paper.
2. Prepare the Puff Pastry: Roll out the puff pastry to fit the roasting tin. Transfer it to the prepared tin and prick the base with a fork, leaving a small border unpricked. This will help the center of the pastry to stay flat while the edges puff up.
3. Cheese Mixture: In a mixing bowl, combine the ricotta or cream cheese, minced garlic, lemon zest, salt, and pepper. Mix until smooth and spreadable.
4. Assemble: Spread the cheese mixture evenly over the puff pastry, leaving the small border untouched. Arrange the asparagus spears on top, either in parallel lines or in a random pattern. Drizzle with olive oil.
5. Bake: Place the roasting tin in the preheated oven and bake for 15-20 minutes, or until the pastry is golden and the asparagus is tender but still vibrant green.
6. Serve: Once baked, remove from the oven and sprinkle with grated Parmesan cheese (if using). Garnish with fresh herbs. Slice and serve warm.

ALTERNATIVE

- Flavor Boost: Add caramelized onions or sun-dried tomatoes beneath the asparagus for added depth of flavor.
- Other Veggies: Try thinly sliced bell peppers, cherry tomatoes, or zucchini instead of asparagus.
- Vegan Version: Use a vegan puff pastry and replace the cheese with a vegan alternative.

CHEESY EGGPLANT PARMESAN STACKS

Indulge in the bright, earthy flavors of asparagus showcased on a flaky pastry base. Adapting this classic springtime favorite for the roasting tin not only simplifies the process but also results in a beautifully presented dish that's perfect for any meal or occasion.

 ## INGREDIENTS

 ## STEPS

- 1 large eggplant, sliced into 1/2-inch rounds (about 8 slices)
- 1/2 cup breadcrumbs
- 1/4 cup grated Parmesan cheese
- 1 large egg, beaten
- 1/2 cup marinara sauce
- 1/2 cup shredded mozzarella cheese
- 1 tsp dried basil (or 2 tbsp fresh basil, chopped)
- 1 tsp dried oregano
- Salt and pepper, to taste
- Olive oil, for drizzling
- Fresh basil leaves, for garnish

1. Preheat oven to 400°F (200°C). Grease roasting tin.
2. Mix breadcrumbs, Parmesan, salt, pepper, basil, oregano.
3. Dip eggplant in beaten egg, coat with breadcrumbs.
4. Arrange in tin, drizzle with olive oil. Bake 15-20 mins, flipping.
5. Add marinara, mozzarella to half, stack, bake 10 mins.
6. Garnish with basil. Serve hot with salad or pasta.

ALTERNATIVE

- Gluten-Free: Use gluten-free breadcrumbs.
- Vegan Option: Swap out traditional cheeses for plant-based alternatives.
- Add Protein: Add a layer of ground turkey or beef sautéed with garlic and onions for a meatier version.

ROASTED BUTTERNUT SQUASH RISOTTO

Delight in a rich and creamy risotto, infused with the earthy sweetness of roasted butternut squash. Adapting this classic dish for the roasting tin simplifies the usually labor-intensive process of making risotto, while preserving its luxurious texture and depth of flavor.

 ## INGREDIENTS

 ## STEPS

- 1 small butternut squash, peeled, seeded, and diced into 1-inch cubes
- 1 cup Arborio rice
- 2 1/2 cups vegetable or chicken stock, warm
- 1/2 small onion, finely chopped
- 2 garlic cloves, minced
- 1/4 cup white wine (optional)
- 1/4 cup freshly grated Parmesan cheese
- 2 tbsp unsalted butter
- 1 tbsp olive oil
- Salt and pepper, to taste
- Fresh sage or parsley, finely chopped, for garnish

1. Preheat oven to 400°F (200°C). Toss squash with oil, salt, pepper, roast 20-25 mins. Set aside.
2. Reduce oven to 375°F (190°C). Combine rice, onion, garlic, butter, and wine (if using) in the roasting tin. Stir.
3. Pour 2 cups warm stock, cover with foil, bake 20 mins.
4. Stir in roasted squash, add more stock if dry, and half the Parmesan.
5. Bake uncovered 10-15 mins until creamy.
6. Season, top with remaining Parmesan, sage/parsley, serve.

ALTERNATIVE

- Vegan Option: Use vegan butter and substitute the Parmesan with nutritional yeast or vegan cheese.
- Protein Boost: Add roasted chicken chunks or sautéed shrimp to the finished risotto for added protein.d
- Additional Veggies: Incorporate roasted bell peppers or sautéed spinach for an extra veggie kick.

LENTIL AND VEGETABLE SHEPHERD'S PIE

Indulge in a comforting classic with a vegetarian twist. This shepherd's pie boasts a hearty lentil and vegetable filling, crowned with a golden layer of roasted garlic mashed potatoes. Using a roasting tin not only ensures an even cook but also creates a delightful crust around the edges.

INGREDIENTS

- 3/4 cup green or brown lentils, rinsed and drained
- 2 medium potatoes, peeled and diced
- 3 cloves garlic, left whole with skin on
- 1 carrot, diced
- 1 celery stalk, diced
- 1/2 onion, finely chopped
- 2 cups vegetable stock
- 1/4 cup green peas
- 2 tbsp tomato paste
- 2 tbsp unsalted butter
- 1/4 cup milk or cream
- 1 tbsp olive oil
- Salt and pepper, to taste
- Fresh parsley, chopped for garnish

STEPS

1. Simmer lentils in vegetable stock for 20-25 mins, drain, set aside.
2. Roast garlic cloves in olive oil at 400°F (200°C) for 10 mins, then squeeze out.
3. Boil potatoes until tender, mash with roasted garlic, butter, milk/cream, salt, and pepper.
4. In the same tin, sauté onions, carrots, celery. Add lentils, tomato paste, peas, salt, and pepper. Spread in the tin.
5. Layer mashed potatoes on top.
6. Bake at 375°F (190°C) for 20-25 mins until golden brown.
7. Sprinkle with fresh chopped parsley before serving.

ALTERNATIVE

- Creamier Mash: Add some grated cheese into the mashed potatoes for a richer flavor.
- Additional Veggies: You can incorporate other vegetables like corn, green beans, or diced bell peppers to the filling.
- Vegan Option: Use plant-based milk and butter for the mashed potatoes.

MEDITERRANEAN VEGGIE AND HALLOUMI BAKE

Transport yourself to the shores of the Mediterranean with this delightful vegetable and halloumi bake. Roasting in a tin infuses the veggies with the savory taste of halloumi and aromatic herbs, making for a delectably hearty dish.

 ## INGREDIENTS

- 150g halloumi cheese, sliced into 1/4-inch thick pieces
- 1 small zucchini, sliced into half-moons
- 1 small red bell pepper, diced
- 1 small yellow bell pepper, diced
- 1/2 red onion, thinly sliced
- 10 cherry tomatoes, halved
- 2 garlic cloves, minced
- 1/4 cup kalamata olives, pitted and sliced
- 3 tbsp olive oil
- 2 tsp dried oregano
- 1 tsp dried basil
- Salt and pepper, to taste
- Fresh basil or parsley, for garnish
- 1/2 lemon, zest and juice

 ## STEPS

1. Preheat oven to 400°F (200°C).
2. Mix zucchini, bell peppers, onion, tomatoes, garlic with olive oil, oregano, basil, salt, and pepper.
3. Spread in roasting tin, add halloumi slices on top.
4. Roast 20-25 mins until veggies are tender and halloumi is golden.
5. Remove, add kalamata olives, lemon zest, lemon juice.
6. Garnish with basil/parsley. Serve with bread or couscous salad.

 ## ALTERNATIVE

- Additional Protein: Add chickpeas or roasted pine nuts to the mix for added crunch and protein.
- Herb Variations: Fresh dill or mint can be used for a different herbaceous note.
- Vegan Version: Replace halloumi with firm tofu slices or vegan cheese. Adjust the roasting time accordingly.

ROASTED BERRY AND MASCARPONE TART

Indulge in this delightful treat that showcases the richness of mascarpone cheese complemented by the sweetness of roasted summer berries. Crafted for the roasting tin, this tart offers a touch of elegance with the simplicity of everyday baking.

 ## INGREDIENTS

- 1 sheet of puff pastry, halved
- 1/2 cup mascarpone cheese
- 1 tbsp honey or maple syrup
- 1/2 tsp vanilla extract
- 1/2 cup mixed summer berries (like raspberries, blueberries, and strawberries)
- 1 tbsp granulated sugar
- Powdered sugar, for dusting
- Fresh mint leaves, for garnish

 ## STEPS

1. Roasting Tin Preparation: Preheat your oven to 375°F (190°C). Lay the halved puff pastry sheet onto the roasting tin lined with parchment paper.
2. Mascarpone Mixture: In a bowl, mix the mascarpone cheese with honey and vanilla extract until smooth. Spread this mixture over the puff pastry, leaving a small border around the edges.
3. Berry Topping: Scatter the mixed berries over the mascarpone layer. Sprinkle the granulated sugar on top.
4. Bake the Tart: Place the roasting tin in the oven and bake for 20-25 minutes, or until the edges of the pastry are golden brown and the berries have released their juices.
5. Cool and Serve: Once out of the oven, let the tart cool slightly. Dust with powdered sugar, garnish with fresh mint leaves, and serve while still warm.

 ## ALTERNATIVE

- Chocolate Drizzle: Melt some dark chocolate and drizzle over the top for an added layer of decadence.
- Nutty Touch: Add a sprinkle of chopped toasted almonds or hazelnuts for a delightful crunch.
- Citrus Zest: Grate some lemon or orange zest into the mascarpone mixture for a hint of citrusy brightness.

STICKY CINNAMON BUN BAKE

Experience the irresistible allure of fresh cinnamon buns without the fuss of individual rolling. This roasting tin version brings you all the warmth and sweetness of traditional cinnamon buns but with a streamlined preparation.

 ## INGREDIENTS

- 1/2 package of store-bought pizza dough or bread dough
- 2 tbsp unsalted butter, melted
- 3 tbsp brown sugar
- 2 tsp ground cinnamon
- 1/4 cup chopped pecans or walnuts (optional)

For the Glaze:
- 1/4 cup powdered sugar
- 1-2 tbsp milk
- 1/2 tsp vanilla extract

 ## STEPS

1. Preheat oven to 375°F (190°C). Grease roasting tin or use parchment paper.
2. Roll out dough into a rectangle. Brush with melted butter.
3. Sprinkle brown sugar, cinnamon, and nuts (if using) evenly.
4. Roll dough tightly, cut into 4 pieces, and place in tin, cut side up.
5. Bake 25-30 mins until golden.
6. Mix powdered sugar, milk, vanilla for glaze. Drizzle on warm buns.
7. Serve warm.

 ## ALTERNATIVE

- Fruity Fill: Add a layer of raisins or dried cranberries before rolling for a fruity twist.
- Cream Cheese Frosting: Replace the simple glaze with a rich cream cheese frosting for an indulgent touch.
- Spice Variation: Introduce a pinch of ground nutmeg or cardamom alongside the cinnamon for a deeper flavor profile.

ACHOCOLATE AND HAZELNUT BROWNIE BARS BUN BAKE

Immerse yourself in a world of rich chocolate and roasted hazelnuts with these roasting tin brownie bars. Perfectly chewy with a hint of crunch, these treats are both indulgent and easy to prepare.

 ## INGREDIENTS

- 60g dark chocolate, roughly chopped
- 40g unsalted butter
- 50g granulated sugar
- 1 large egg
- 30g all-purpose flour
- 2 tbsp unsweetened cocoa powder
- 1/4 tsp baking powder
- 1/4 tsp salt
- 30g roasted hazelnuts, coarsely chopped
- 1 tsp vanilla extract

 ## STEPS

1. Preheat oven to 350°F (175°C). Line tin with parchment paper.
2. Melt dark chocolate and butter (microwave or double boiler).
3. Whisk in sugar, vanilla, and egg.
4. Sift flour, cocoa, baking powder, salt, fold into chocolate mixture.
5. Add chopped hazelnuts.
6. Spread batter in tin, bake 15-20 mins until toothpick has few crumbs.
7. Cool 10 mins in tin, lift using parchment paper, cut into bars, and serve.

 ## ALTERNATIVE

- Double Chocolate: For an even richer flavor, fold in some chocolate chips or chunks before baking.
- Nut Variations: Swap out the hazelnuts for other nuts like almonds or pecans.
- Fruity Touch: Introduce dried cherries or cranberries for a contrasting tartness.

PEACH AND ALMOND CRUMBLE

Indulge in the warmth of summer flavors with this roasting tin peach and almond crumble. Succulent peaches topped with a golden almond-studded topping make for a delectable dessert that's simple to put together.

 ## INGREDIENTS

- 2 large ripe peaches, pitted and sliced
- 30g granulated sugar, divided
- 1 tsp lemon juice
- 1/2 tsp vanilla extract
- 40g all-purpose flour
- 25g cold unsalted butter, diced
- 20g rolled oats
- 20g almond flakes
- 1/4 tsp ground cinnamon

 ## STEPS

1. Roasting Tin Preparation: Preheat your oven to 375°F (190°C). Grease your roasting tin lightly or line with parchment paper.
2. Peach Layer: In a mixing bowl, combine sliced peaches, half of the sugar, lemon juice, and vanilla extract. Toss to coat evenly, then spread the peach slices at the bottom of the prepared roasting tin.
3. Prepare Crumble: In a separate bowl, mix together flour, rolled oats, almond flakes, remaining sugar, and cinnamon. Add in the cold, diced butter and use your fingers or a pastry cutter to blend until the mixture resembles coarse breadcrumbs.
4. Assemble and Bake: Sprinkle the crumble topping evenly over the peaches in the roasting tin. Bake for 25-30 minutes or until the crumble is golden brown and the peach juices are bubbling.
5. Serve: Allow the crumble to cool slightly before serving. It pairs wonderfully with vanilla ice cream or whipped cream.

 ## ALTERNATIVE

- Mixed Fruit Crumble: You can mix in other fruits like berries or apricots with the peaches for a varied flavor.
- Nutty Variations: If almonds aren't your favorite, try using pecans or walnuts in the crumble.
- Spice it Up: Add a touch of nutmeg or ginger for a warming spice kick.

COCONUT AND LIME BREAD PUDDING

This tropical twist on a classic bread pudding brings the zesty flavor of lime together with the richness of coconut. Prepared in a roasting tin, it's a delightful dessert that will transport you straight to a beachside paradise.

 ## INGREDIENTS

- 4 slices of day-old bread (preferably brioche or challah), cut into 1-inch cubes
- 1 cup coconut milk
- 1/4 cup granulated sugar
- 1 large egg
- 1 tbsp lime zest
- 2 tbsp lime juice
- 1/4 tsp vanilla extract
- Pinch of salt
- 2 tbsp shredded coconut, for topping
- Fresh lime slices and whipped cream, for serving

 ## STEPS

1. Roasting Tin Preparation: Preheat your oven to 350°F (175°C). Grease your roasting tin lightly or line with parchment paper.
2. Bread Layering: Place the cubed bread pieces evenly in the prepared roasting tin.
3. Pudding Mixture: In a mixing bowl, whisk together coconut milk, sugar, egg, lime zest, lime juice, vanilla extract, and a pinch of salt until smooth.
4. Assemble: Pour the coconut-lime mixture over the bread cubes, ensuring that all pieces are soaked. Allow it to sit for about 10 minutes so the bread can absorb the liquid.
5. Top and Bake: Sprinkle the shredded coconut over the top. Bake for 25-30 minutes or until the pudding is set and the top has a light golden color.
6. Serve: Allow the bread pudding to cool slightly in the roasting tin. Serve warm with fresh lime slices and a dollop of whipped cream.

 ## ALTERNATIVE

- Add Fruit: Incorporate some fresh pineapple chunks or mango slices into the pudding before baking for added tropical flavor.
- Crunch Factor: Toasted chopped macadamia nuts or almonds sprinkled on top can offer a delightful crunch.
- Spice it Up: For a subtle kick, add a pinch of ground cardamom or a drizzle of rum to the mixture.

SHEPHERD'S PIE

The timeless British classic, Shepherd's Pie, is brought to your table with a roasting tin twist. Layered with seasoned minced meat and vegetables and crowned with velvety mashed potatoes, this is comfort food at its finest.

 ## INGREDIENTS

- 250g lamb or beef mince
- 1 medium onion, finely chopped
- 1 carrot, diced
- 1 celery stalk, diced
- 2 garlic cloves, minced
- 150ml beef or vegetable stock
- 1 tbsp tomato paste
- 1 tsp Worcestershire sauce
- 2 medium potatoes, peeled and diced
- 50ml milk
- 2 tbsp unsalted butter
- Salt and pepper, to taste
- Fresh parsley, chopped (for garnish)

 ## STEPS

1. Roasting Tin Preparation: Preheat your oven to 375°F (190°C).
2. Potato Topping: In a pot, boil the potatoes until tender. Drain and mash with milk, butter, salt, and pepper until smooth. Set aside.
3. Meat Filling: In a skillet over medium heat, brown the mince, breaking it up with a spoon. Add onions, carrots, celery, and garlic and cook until the vegetables soften.
4. Stir in the tomato paste, Worcestershire sauce, and stock. Let it simmer until the mixture thickens. Season with salt and pepper.
5. Assemble in Roasting Tin: Pour the meat mixture into the base of the roasting tin. Carefully spread the mashed potatoes over the top, using a fork to create a ridged pattern.
6. Bake: Place the roasting tin in the preheated oven and bake for 20-25 minutes or until the top is golden and the filling is bubbling.
7. Serve: Let it cool for a few minutes, then sprinkle with fresh parsley before serving.

 ## ALTERNATIVE

- Cheese Crown: Sprinkle some grated cheddar on top of the mashed potatoes before baking for a cheesy crust.
- Veggie Boost: Add green peas or diced mushrooms to the meat mixture for extra flavor and texture.
- Herb Infusion: Mix some chopped rosemary or thyme into the meat mixture for a herby touch.

TOAD IN THE HOLE

Dive into British culinary tradition with this Toad in the Hole, an iconic dish that combines sausages with a savory pudding batter. Using a roasting tin, we recreate this classic while ensuring crispy edges and fluffy centers.

 ## INGREDIENTS

- 4 quality sausages
- 70g all-purpose flour
- 1 large egg
- 100ml milk
- Pinch of salt
- 2 tbsp vegetable oil or lard
- 1 tsp fresh thyme leaves (optional)
- Freshly ground black pepper, to taste

 ## STEPS

1. Roasting Tin Preparation: Preheat your oven to 425°F (220°C). Add the vegetable oil or lard to the roasting tin and place it in the oven to heat up.
2. Batter Making: In a mixing bowl, whisk together the flour, salt, and a pinch of black pepper. Make a well in the center and crack in the egg. Gradually add the milk, whisking continuously, to form a smooth batter. Let the batter rest for at least 15 minutes.
3. Sausages in Tin: Carefully remove the hot roasting tin from the oven. Place the sausages in the tin, ensuring they're spaced apart. Return to the oven for about 10 minutes until the sausages are browned.
4. Pouring the Batter: Once the sausages are browned, quickly pour the batter over them. Sprinkle with thyme leaves if using.
5. Bake: Place the roasting tin back in the oven and bake for 25-30 minutes or until the batter is risen, golden, and crispy.
6. Serve: Serve immediately, ideally with onion gravy and vegetables on the side.

ALTERNATIVE

- Herby Twist: Incorporate chopped rosemary or sage into the batter for an aromatic boost.
- Spicy Kick: Use spicy sausages or add a pinch of chili flakes to the batter for a touch of heat.
- Vegetarian Alternative: Replace traditional sausages with vegetarian sausages, but adjust cooking time as needed based on the sausage instructions.

71

CORNISH PASTY BAKE

A tribute to the beloved Cornish pasty, this bake takes the key ingredients from the iconic snack and adapts them to a hearty, roasting tin version. Experience the rich flavors of beef, potatoes, and vegetables, all embraced by a flaky crust.

 ## INGREDIENTS

- 200g beef skirt or stewing steak, cut into small cubes
- 1 medium potato, peeled and diced into small cubes
- 1 small onion, finely chopped
- 1 small swede (rutabaga), peeled and diced into small cubes
- Salt and freshly ground black pepper, to taste
- 1 tsp fresh thyme leaves, chopped
- 2 tbsp beef stock or water
- 1 sheet of ready-rolled puff pastry
- 1 egg, lightly beaten (for egg wash)

 ## STEPS

1. Roasting Tin Preparation: Preheat your oven to 400°F (200°C). Lightly grease your roasting tin.
2. Filling Prep: In a large mixing bowl, combine the beef, potato, onion, swede, thyme, salt, and pepper. Toss well to ensure all ingredients are evenly seasoned.
3. Assembling in Tin: Spread the beef and vegetable mixture evenly in the roasting tin. Drizzle with the beef stock or water.
4. Pastry Layer: Unroll the puff pastry sheet and lay it over the top of the beef and vegetable mixture in the tin, tucking in the edges. Brush the surface with the beaten egg to give it a golden finish when baked.
5. Bake: Place the roasting tin in the oven and bake for 25-30 minutes or until the pastry is risen, golden brown, and the filling is bubbly and cooked through.
6. Serve: Let it sit for a few minutes before serving. Use a sharp knife or pizza cutter to divide into portions.

ALTERNATIVE

- Herb Infusion: Add a mix of herbs such as rosemary, sage, or parsley for added depth of flavor.
- Cheese Top: Before sealing with the puff pastry, sprinkle some grated cheddar or mozzarella on top for a cheesy twist.
- Vegetarian Pasty: Substitute beef with a mixture of mushrooms, lentils, and additional vegetables. Adjust seasoning accordingly.

ETON MESS

A delightful twist on the classic British dessert, Eton Mess. In this version, we roast the strawberries to intensify their flavors, which pairs beautifully with the crispy meringues and creamy whipped cream.

 ## INGREDIENTS

- 300g fresh strawberries, hulled and halved
- 2 tbsp granulated sugar
- 1 tsp vanilla extract
- 100g meringue nests, roughly broken into pieces
- 200ml heavy whipping cream
- 1 tbsp confectioners' sugar
- Fresh mint leaves for garnish (optional)

 ## STEPS

1. Roasting the Strawberries: Preheat your oven to 350°F (175°C). In the roasting tin, mix the strawberries with granulated sugar and vanilla extract. Roast in the oven for 15-20 minutes or until the strawberries are soft and release their juices. Allow to cool slightly in the tin.
2. Whipping the Cream: While the strawberries are cooling, in a mixing bowl, whip the heavy cream with the confectioners' sugar until it forms soft peaks.
3. Assembling: Once the strawberries have slightly cooled, fold the meringue pieces into the strawberries, ensuring you mix in some of the delicious juices. Gently fold in the whipped cream, creating a marbled effect with the strawberry juices.
4. Serve: Spoon the Eton Mess into serving bowls. You can garnish with fresh mint leaves for an added touch of freshness.

 ## ALTERNATIVE

- Berry Variation: You can mix in or replace strawberries with other berries like raspberries, blackberries, or blueberries.
- Chocolatey Twist: Drizzle a bit of melted dark chocolate or sprinkle some cocoa nibs for a contrasting taste.
- Tropical Flavor: Roast some passion fruits or pineapples along with strawberries for a tropical variation of the classic Eton Mess.

TIPS AND TRICKS

ROASTING TIPS:

- Even Sizing: When roasting vegetables or meats, ensure pieces are uniformly sized to guarantee even cooking.
- Preheat the Oven: Always preheat your oven. Placing your dish in an oven that hasn't reached its set temperature can alter cooking times.
- Roasting Rack: Using a roasting rack can help circulate air around the meat, ensuring an even roast and a crispy outer layer.
- Temperature Probe: For meats, investing in a good temperature probe can help you identify when your roast has reached perfection.
- Resting Time: Once roasted, always let meats rest before slicing. This allows juices to redistribute, ensuring a succulent roast.
- Oil Wisely: Different oils have different smoke points. For high-temperature roasting, opt for oils like avocado, grapeseed, or canola which have higher smoke points.
- Season Generously: Unlike other methods, roasting can handle and often requires generous seasoning. Don't be shy with those herbs and spices!

GENERAL COOKING TIPS:

- Mise en Place: This French term means "everything in its place". Before starting, gather all your ingredients and utensils. It streamlines the cooking process and reduces stress.
- Clean As You Go: Maintain a clean workspace. It not only makes the process more enjoyable but also ensures safety.
- Sharp Knives: A sharp knife isn't just efficient, it's also safer. It requires less force and reduces the chance of slipping.
- Taste as You Cook: This is the key to understanding and enhancing flavors. Adjust seasonings gradually as you cook.
- Start with a Hot Pan: When sautéing or frying, let your pan heat up before adding oil. This ensures a good sear.
- Use Quality Ingredients: Fresh, quality ingredients can elevate a dish significantly. Where possible, source locally and seasonally.
- Read the Recipe: Before starting, read through the entire recipe. Familiarizing yourself with the steps can prevent mistakes and oversights.
- Stay Organized: Whether it's arranging ingredients in the order of use or keeping frequently used utensils within arm's reach, an organized kitchen can significantly speed up the cooking process.
- Learn from Mistakes: Everyone makes mistakes in the kitchen, even seasoned chefs. What's crucial is to learn and adapt. Over time, these experiences become valuable lessons.

Enjoy the Process: Cooking is as much about the journey as the outcome. Relish the process, from the chop of the knife to the sizzle in the pan. Embrace the creativity and sensory pleasures it brings.

Join us on your favorite platform .
scan the Qr code on your phone or tablet.

Printed in Great Britain
by Amazon